THE VICTORIAN HEROINE

THE VICTORIAN HEROINE

A CHANGING IDEAL
1837-1873

BY

PATRICIA THOMSON

LONDON
OXFORD UNIVERSITY PRESS
NEW YORK TORONTO
1956

Oxford University Press, Amen House, London E.C.4
GLASGOW NEW YORK TORONTO MELBOURNE WELLINGTON
BOMBAY CALCUTTA MADRAS KARACHI
CAPE TOWN IBADAN NAIROBI ACCRA SINGAPORE

PRINTED IN GREAT BRITAIN

CONTENTS

PROLOGUE

LONG before the days of that Victorian best-seller, *The Woman Who Did*, and a full half century before *Ann Veronica*, the novel was sensitive to the significant changes that were taking place in the position of women. By the time that writers at the close of the century 'took up' the topic of women's emancipation, it had been so much discussed that novelists and reading public alike were conditioned to the idea of the New Woman. As far as she was concerned, the initial stages of Victorian surprise were over. Novelists might approve or disapprove, proselytise or attack, but in either case they dealt with her, deliberately, as a social phenomenon. As such, she appears a remote, documentary figure to us today. If we sympathise with her ardours and her tribulations, we do so with our minds. For our hearts to be touched we must look further back, to the time when all-embracing feminism had not yet cut her off from the rest of her sex, when she was still an individual and not a representative of a system, when feminist doctrines were making their impact for the first time on both the Victorian woman and the Victorian novel-heroine.

In these earlier novels of the Victorian age, we find that the feminist impress, although fainter, is far more fascinating. It is here that we can observe the insidious percolation, often against the author's will, of the new ideas that were beginning to undermine the Victorian domestic idyll. It was not so easy, then, as it was for authors, later, to decide on which side of the fence they would sit, for the fence was only in the process of construction. It was the age of the social novel and the different, particular aspects of feminism interested the novelist—just as they interested the contemporary Victorian woman. The self-conscious aphorisms of a Meredith heroine were still far in the distance and would have meant little to the average reader. 'Women have passed Seraglio Point but have not yet rounded Cape Turk.' What charm had a generalisation like that compared with the concrete delights of heroines who were 'going in for' Good

Works, or expressing their approval of the notion of Lectures to
Ladies? It is precisely this warmth and feeling of imminence that
makes worthwhile a study of the interplay between fact and fiction in the Victorian novel. The Victorian woman and the
Victorian novel-heroine present interesting and, at times, illuminating companion pictures as they move slowly towards emancipation.

Boundary dates, in such a survey as this, are always arbitrary
affairs. As, by 1873 (which also marked the death of one of the
most distinguished of feminists, John Stuart Mill) almost every
important emancipation movement had been set afoot, that year
will mark the closing point of the period. But although 1837, the
date of the young Queen's accession, seems to provide a good
starting point, the reader may well wonder why it should be preferred to 1792, the year that gave the feminist movement unwilling birth, with the publication of Mary Wollstonecraft's
Vindication of the Rights of Women. Sufficient reason is found in
the reception given to that document when it first appeared.

To Mary Wollstonecraft the time must have appeared ripe for
the delivery of her feminist doctrines; the French Revolution
should by now have prepared the nation for far more sweeping
reforms than those she was about to advocate on behalf of
women. And, indeed, had her pamphlet been published a year
or two earlier it is unlikely that it would have been held up to the
same ridicule. As it was, she was just a little too late. England was
in the grip of anti-Jacobin fear: radicalism had given way to a
reactionary policy of repression: Englishmen, distrusting the
terrorism that Liberty had brought to France, had two new
watchwords, Patriotism and Religion. In the years that followed,
the Evangelicals, in particular—the Saints of Clapham—began
to feel their power as the sphere of their activities widened. It
was remarkable how readily the nation responded to guidance.
By 1804 indeed, when the Bible Society was formed, it might
almost have seemed as if Sabbath observance and foreign missions had always been part of England's heritage and as if it had
been another country altogether that fifteen years before had
stood on the brink of revolution.

In such circumstances, we cannot marvel that the *Vindication*
should have met with little encouragement. The child of revolu-

tionary unrest could not be expected to thrive in a Sunday School environment. The tide of public opinion had turned and was flowing steadily back to the shores of stability: and, above the surge of the retreating waves, only a few devotees and her faithful Godwin strained their ears to catch her heartfelt cry—'Let woman share the rights and she will emulate the virtues of man.'

The courage of Mary Wollstonecraft was equalled only by her tactlessness. It was a *sine qua non* that she should incur the derision of men but it was unfortunate that she should also have alienated her own sex. For, although she had vision enough to see what women might be, she had not tolerance enough to forgive them for what they were; and women, whom she dismissed impatiently in the *Vindication* as 'gentle domestic brutes', were unlikely to consider that she had placed them under any obligation to lend her their warm support. She was not, however, content with ridiculing women's ignorance, their utilitarian attitude to virtue, their taste for pleasure, their snobbery of rank and riches or their carefully cultivated myth of feminine delicacy. She went on painstakingly to show how they could be improved out of all recognition by the simple expedient of giving them co-education, economic independence, legal equality and free access to the salaried professions.

From such a drastic programme, women of all classes recoiled in dismay. Mrs. Sarah Trimmer repressively summed up, on behalf of the happily married, after she had scanned the *Vindication*: 'Of "The Rights of Women" I can say nothing but that I found so much happiness in having a husband to assist me in forming a proper judgement, and in taking upon him the chief labour of providing for a family, that I never wished for a further degree of liberty or consequence than I enjoyed.'

Mrs. Trimmer, Sunday School superintendent, writer of educational books for children and the mother of twelve, showed comfortable disregard for those who had neither her advantages, her responsibilities nor her Dr. Trimmer. But her bland detachment is not untypical of her sex at that time; even the educated had not been trained to look upon generalisations and theorising without alarm. The *Vindication* demanded too much of women to whom taking a 'broad view' seemed as unladylike and as much out of their province as a broad jump, and who shrank from consideration of any but the particular case. The popular ideal of women is best revealed in Dr. Gregory's *Legacy to my Daughters* (1774) which was acclaimed with such enthusiasm that it was reprinted at intervals throughout the next hundred years. His initial postulate, which prepared his daughters for the worst, was that woman's life was, more often than not, one of suffering. Consequently, in the event of their husband's infidelity their sole redress would be found in the consolations of religion. And as their principal virtues, in men's eyes, were humility, modesty, chastity, delicacy and beauty their main care should be—in the event of having health, to conceal it; of having wit and good sense, to suppress them; of having learning, to keep it a profound secret. Such was the pocket testament of a young lady in the reign of George III: such was the creed which gave to the *Vindication* the semblance of a blast of heresy.

But, quite apart from the revolutionary air that the feminist doctrines wore, the excessive enthusiasm and sensibility that they displayed jarred upon women who might otherwise have lent them a sympathetic ear. Sensibility, in 1792, was on its way out; feminism not yet on its way in. When Jane Austen levelled a mocking pen at excess of sensibility in novel heroines she was in complete sympathy with the spirit of the age as Mary Wollstonecraft was not. Radical in her views and retrograde in her emotions, the latter met with a reception from her own sex that could scarcely be called encouraging. The energy liberated by her new, ennobling ideas was not lost, as could be seen half a century later—but her contemporary influence upon literature and life was slight. The bond that united reasonable women at the close of the eighteenth century was not desire for freedom but dislike of over-emotionalism of any sort. Women were not to be extracted from the quagmire of sensibility all at once— and until they were they felt ready for neither independence nor equality. A transitional period, in short, in which reason, intelligence and good sense assumed importance for women, was necessary to ensure that they would be in a fit state to use their liberty wisely.

The accession of a female sovereign—'a charming invention', as Miss Eden kindly called it—saw this interim period drawing to a close. In the years between, the adamant soil of public opinion had been insensibly prepared for the sowings of feminism. In intellectual circles there had been considerable discussion of feminist aims, while the sphere of the middle-class woman had gradually been widened to include a certain amount of home-education and philanthropy on a slightly more organised scale than the earlier bowl-of-soup-and-a-tract tradition. And, in literature, the social novel was just beginning its sturdy edging-out of the novel of fashion from public favour—an important development, for with the social novel began that definite co-relation between the Victorian woman and the Victorian heroine which is the theme of this book. I am interested principally in assessing the effect of the feminist movement on the heroine of the novel, in indicating how far the novelists' ideal of womanhood was affected by contemporary trends. There are already too many excellent factual histories of the feminist cause for me to do more than give a feminist backbone to each chapter—which is then supplied with substance from the novels themselves.

CHAPTER I

Good Works

1. CHARITABLE DICTATORS

OF all the aspects of feminism that confronted Victorians it was philanthropy that caused them least alarm. For although the philanthropic movement which broke over the feminine world of the '50's and '60's owed its initial energy to the work of various outstanding women, it would not have increased so steadily in force and importance had its doctrines not been of general appeal.

It is the social, rather than the legal, position of women in 1837 and the years following, that explains the significant part taken by philanthropy in their lives. On paper, the position of the Victorian wife was discouraging. She could neither own property nor make a will, keep her own savings nor claim any of her husband's. By marriage she lost her identity in his and consequently had no power over her children and no grounds for divorce. The position, however, was seldom put on paper. So that the vast, contented majority of wives remained ignorantly unruffled by their legal non-existence and single women, for the most part, felt their economic disabilities more keenly than married women their legal impotence. For although single women possessed the legal privilege of retaining their own earnings, they were, in the lower classes, at starvation level and, in the middle, just sufficient to ensure depressing indigence.

So much for the legal status of women. What of their position, in fact? . . . Only the upper classes were inoculated, with self-satisfaction, against uneasiness. The *Court Magazine* of 1837 indicated as much in tones of calm conviction:

It is not only in times of peril that we find the superiority of the British female aristocracy apparent. It is in the habits of their ordinary life, in the privacy of their family circle and in their sphere of domestic charities that we find English ladies holding unquestionably the highest rank among civilised nations.[1]

The complacency of the Lady was counter-poised, at the other end of the scale, by the resignation of the working woman. The transference of work from the house to the factory had brought only long hours, small pay and heavy drudgery: masculine resentment of the monopoly of female labour had completely dissipated the Peterloo sense of comradeship; and now, well-meaning Evangelicals were attempting to take her subsistence from her by limiting the number of hours she could work. Neither her husband's resentment nor Lord Ashley's solicitude roused the working woman from her state of settled dejection and not even the female aristocracy was less inclined towards thoughts of further emancipation.

But, in the middle classes, where women were burdened with neither an excess of privileges nor privations, there was a vague sensation of discontent and emptiness. The daughter of the house was considerably better educated than she had ever been before. Fashionable schools* existed which offered a curriculum of Music, Dancing, Art, German, Italian, French, English, Morals and Religion; and even with the stress laid, in as costly and pretentious a manner possible, on the accomplishments, the tail end of the curriculum was bound to come in for occasional notice. In intellectual families, the daughter continued her education under the guidance of a father or a brother and, in such cases, a remarkable amount of home-reading and learning— of Latin, Greek and philosophy, among other things—did go on. Without such help, if she had enough determination, she pursued her studies alone; if not, she relapsed into a young-lady life of visiting, novel-reading, gossiping and embroidering.

Up to this time, such a way of life had naturally terminated on marriage, and household management had left little time for ennui. But, with the increased prosperity of the middle classes, housewifery had been relegated to servants and had fallen into disrepute. So that now, not only the marriageable girls in a house but also its mistress were casting helplessly around for something to do, something to occupy their vacant hours—something, however, that would not detract from their new standing as Middle-

* This was the curriculum offered by the school to which Frances Cobbe went in 1836. The charge for two years was £1,000.

Class Ladies. Employment in the great world was, of course, out
of the question. The existence of 'a great and invidious distinction drawn between working and professional women' was painstakingly made clear by Harriet Martineau in her novel *Deerbrook*:

'Can you not tell me of some way in which a woman may earn
money?'

'A woman? What rate of woman? Do you mean yourself? That
question is easily answered. A woman from the uneducated classes
can get a subsistence by washing and cooking, by milking cows or
going to service and in some parts of the kingdom by working in a
cotton mill or burnishing plate. . . . But, for an educated woman, a
woman with the powers which God gave her religiously improved,
with a reason which lays life open before her, an understanding
which surveys science as its appropriate task and a conscience which
would make every species of responsibility safe—for such a woman
there is in all England no chance of subsistence but by teaching—
that almost ineffectual teaching which can never countervail the
education of circumstances and for which but one in a thousand is
fit—or by being a superior Miss Nares—the feminine gender of the
tailor and the hatter.'

'The tutor, tailor and the hatter. Is this all?'

'All; except that there are departments of art and literature from
which it is impossible to shut woman out. These are not however to
be regarded as resources for bread.'[2]

Miss Martineau's modest claim on behalf of her sex for the
possession of a reason which laid life open, an understanding
which surveyed science as its appropriate task or, what was even
more advanced, a mercenary ambition to earn money, was not
one acknowledged by many women. But they were, none the less,
sufficiently aware of the aimlessness of their new existence to
seize eagerly upon the extra-mural interest of charitable work,
however vaguely defined its limits still were. In 1837, work parties
and district visiting among the poor, in not too squalid districts,
were the most popular forms of benevolence. Since the Evangelicals had provided opposition to feudal bounty, most female
works of charity had a religious colouring. And although it was
Non-conformist and Unitarian families that provided the core of
the later philanthropic movement, in such mild activities as
E. M. Sewell records all sects took part. 'As regarded the

poor and suffering, both Church and people and dissenters worked together—on the whole amiably—in Benevolent societies working parties where reading aloud was the order of the day.'[3]

Plain sewing for the poor, even to the enlivening accompaniment of extracts from *Tracts for the Times* or *The Christian Observer*, may have had nothing specially adventurous about it but it was at least an organised effort. Such female charities received masculine countenance but the spirit of the age was, rather, one of individual benevolence. It is not until the later '50's that we find benevolence, as represented in Dickens, largely replaced by philanthropy and referred to by Walter Bagehot as 'an out-moded taste'. According to a contemporary observer, W. R. Greg, this new spirit was not only the product of growing leisure and prosperity but also of fear. During the '30's and '40's, while women sought charitable work out of boredom, men became liberal-handed out of fear; fear of an epidemic prompted the Public Health and Sanitary Reports; fear of revolution provoked solicitude for the conditions of the working classes. But, at the same time, the middle classes experienced a more pleasurable sensation—the power of patronage —and indulged freely in it. All they expected in return was gratitude.

Even, however, when benevolence was most popular, even when the Brothers Cheeryble, Mr. Pickwick, Mr. Brownlow and the reformed Scrooge were most in tune with the times, not all Victorians were prepared to accept Dickens' Christmas philosophy. Between 1840 and 1850 the *Westminster Review* published a series of articles condemning the policy of 'the full purse and never the equal measure', running down 'pseudo-benevolent haranguers' and demanding for the working classes justice not charity. And as the prophet of the cult of personal benevolence Dickens came in for much of their criticism. It seldom happened in actual fact—and certainly never in Dickens—that victims of benevolence were capable of showing as much spirit as Robert Owen's employees, when they walked out of his model factory one morning as a protest against too much compulsory music and dancing.

It is very noticeable in Dickens that benevolence is exclusively

the province of men. There are no large-hearted ladies to set
against the Cheerybles—only the Pusey-ite Mrs. Pardiggle to act
as a sobering reminder to women that officiousness and charity
need not go hand in hand. It was men alone who were considered
capable of making large gestures; women, because of their sex,
could merely do good in a small way. This attitude was especially
marked in 'Church families' where the women had been bred in
an atmosphere of reverent submission to the opinions of their
men-folk. There was as much of a contrast between the Yonge
family and the Martineau family as between the scope of Charlotte's work and that of Harriet's. Charlotte's drastic education
by her father was a very different matter from the spirit of intellectual and religious enquiry shared by the young Martineaus.
Non-conformists were capable of taking the broad view of sex
where important issues were at stake : however great the sacrifice
to their own personal comfort. 'Leave it to other women to make
shirts and darn socks; and do you devote your self to this,' was
brother Thomas Martineau's momentous advice upon the publication of Harriet's first article upon Practical Divinity; and
Harriet saw no reason to demur. The 'shelter of home'—the key
phrase in the anti-feminist angelus—had far less meaning for
the daughter of a dissenting family than for the daughter of
Orthodox parents: to her the home stood rather for a stimulating common background than for a refuge. Consequently, it is
not surprising that the lead in organised philanthropy should
have come from women who had been bred in the tradition of
independent, decided action. Nor that the intrepid step taken by
Mary Carpenter, the first of such women—from her home into
the uncharted dangers of Bristol slum streets—should have been
observed by the Carpenter family with interested approval and
admirable calm.

Her work, and that of other individual women, gradually
assumed the form of a definite movement as the years passed. So
that the exclusive sister charities of 1837, district visiting and
work parties, found themselves by 1873 crowded into a very
subsidiary position in a large family of practical Social Sciences—
such as Ragged School teaching, superintendence of reformatories, Workhouse visiting, Rescue work and Housing and Planning. But in 1835, when Miss Carpenter formed her own working

and visiting society in Bristol, philanthropy had not become a national pastime and there was no beginners' handbook for her to refer to. She was, however, quite sure that all good works must have a plan behind them to be any good at all; so she allotted her lady-visitors particular districts and put her foot down firmly on indiscriminate almsgiving. In the meantime, she taught in Sunday schools—and once she had become aware of the conditions of misery and wretched ignorance among the poor, visiting ceased to content her. In 1846, she not only started her first Ragged School for destitute children in Lewin's Mead but began a Night School in which she extended an amiable welcome to the 'young men and women of the lowest character and most hardened habits' whom she drew from the streets. So that, with industrial classes all day, mid-day distribution of soup (without a tract to aid digestion), night school every evening and Sunday School classes morning, noon and night on the Sabbath, this voluntary, full-time philanthropist found herself exempt at least from the fashionable feminine complaint* of occupational vacuity.

While she was tackling Bristol, the Christian Socialists in London, under the guidance of Kingsley and Maurice, were drawing round them a band of ardent social workers of both sexes. We can gain no indication at all of the underlying enthusiasm and excitement from the prosaic designations by which their activities were known—The Working Men's College, the Ladies' Co-operative Guild, the Working Women's Classes . . . Even from their Society for the Diffusion of Sanitary Knowledge a spirit of adventure could not be said to be absent. Philanthropy, for women in especial, began to assume a welcome aspect; for many it had become an engrossing hobby, for some an entirely new department of activity, for which they felt themselves very well suited. The more advanced even referred to philanthropy as being 'in their line', forgetful of the fact that their lines were supposed to fall in exclusively domestic places. By 1848 Lady Stanley of Alderley was writing with satisfaction

---

* In *A Woman's Thoughts About Women* (1858), Dinah Mulock Craik complained that the chief canker at the root of women's lives was the lack of 'something to do'—but the solution she offered was a renewed interest in housekeeping for married women.

to her husband that she had 'met with a very useful publication, The Family Economist, a penny mag; all in my line, about ventilation and emigration and such like philanthropic pursuits.'[4]

With the ground thus prepared for it, the '50's saw the philanthropic movement properly established. Mary Carpenter concentrated upon juvenile delinquency; wrote a book on reformatories, and instigated a conference of social workers. She herself took no part in the discussion at this although her proposals were made the resolution of the meeting. 'To have lifted up her voice in an assembly of gentlemen would have been as she then felt, tantamount to unsexing herself. Like the Hon. Miss Murray who had been labouring for twenty years in the same cause she sat silent.'*

With the help of Lady Byron she was able to open a reformatory school 'Red Lodge' for delinquent girls, and such were her crowded, endless days of labour, so stoical and spartan her regimen, that she wore down even the robust ebullience of her fellow-philanthropist, Frances Cobbe. The strain of trudging in all weathers from one end of the town to the other, tolerating abuse and rudeness, facing actual dangers in dark, slum streets and remaining optimistic in the face of failure and opposition was indeed considerable; but all this a philanthropist might have endured had her spirit not been broken by Miss Carpenter's lofty contempt for regular meals. To such gastronomical detachment Miss Cobbe was conscious that she could never attain; and in 1859 we find her, as a relaxation from reformatory work, turning her attention to the other new charity of the '50's—workhouse visiting.

This had come into the philanthropic zone, six years before, when Louisa Twining paid the first official visit of a woman to Strand Union workhouse. When she made known her horror at the conditions of dirt, disease, squalid ignorance and vice existing within workhouse walls, the 'privilege of visiting' was denied to other women. But by the next year the visiting system had gradually, though unofficially, extended and, by 1857, little

---

* Mrs. Carpenter suggested a diplomatic reason for her daughter's reserved attitude—'knowing how jealous the lords of creation are of the interference of women . . .'

pamphlets written by well-meaning ladies were making their
appearance, with such pleasing titles as *Sunshine in the Workhouse* or *Christmas Eve in the Workhouse*. These were marked
by a sense of the sharp social division between the visitors and
the inmates; the female gender was not quite big enough to hold
both a workhouse woman and a middle class lady, such as Mrs.
G. H. Sheppard:

I found about ten, wretched degraded-looking women crouching
round the fire—one especially I noticed who had her disfigured, diseased face from me. I went up to them, laid my hand on a shoulder
and said, 'My poor woman, is it true that if I offer to come in and see
you now and then you would treat me with abuse and coldness? Can
this be true of English Women to an English Lady?'[5]

Kindly patronage was not however the extent of the work done
by workhouse visitors. In 1857 the Social Science Association
put forward a proposal that a central society for the promotion
of workhouse visiting should be formed and, from then on, visits
were put on an official basis. It needed some little courage to try
to bring sunshine to such scenes as Frances Cobbe records—to
sick women, lying on wretched beds attended by paupers, to
children with half-blinded, scarred faces, in hideous inadequate
workhouse frocks and heavy hob-nailed boots. But dauntlessly,
amongst such squalor, entered the Visiting Ladies, with their
little packets of good tea, pictures to hang on the walls, canaries
in cages, flowers, fruit and magazines—gifts which, in all their
inadequacy and incongruity, were appreciated. Against what she
considered was the worst scandal of all—the practice of sending
incurables from hospitals to die in misery on hard, workhouse
beds—Frances Cobbe resolutely set her face, and her proposal to
separate incurables from ordinary paupers and provide them
with comforts was finally carried out.

Such were the main activities between 1850 and 1860; but two
other important factors contributed to the changing public attitude towards female philanthropy. The first was the suggestion
put forward by philanthropists themselves that a natural superiority in voluntary, over 'hired', labour did not of necessity exist,
as had always till then been assumed. Octavia Hill, rankling
under the disadvantage of being the salaried secretary, among a

group of 'voluntary ladies', for the Working Women's Classes, had expressed herself freely:

As I am thrown among 'ladies' I hope I may discover good in them —I don't know what there is in the word 'lady' which will connect itself with all the things I despise and hate; first and foremost it suggests a want of perseverance, a bending before small obstacles, a continual 'I would if . . .'[6]

The question of salaries, once raised, was not to be dismissed. Mrs. Jameson, writing in 1855, struck a shrewd blow on behalf of the paid worker by advocating training for women charity workers in hospitals and schools, workhouses and reformatories, followed by a lengthened probation and strict examination, so that women should no longer be 'amateur ladies of charity but brave women whose vocation was fixed'.[7] Philanthropy, which seven years earlier had been daringly referred to as 'a line', was now dignified into a vocation.

The other important sign of the times, from the feminist point of view, was the gesture made in 1857 by the Social Science Association when it opened its membership to women. This not only indicated recognition by men of the scope and purpose of women's work, but also allowed the various feminine movements throughout the country to be linked up, and made possible friendship and co-operation between prominent women philanthropists who would otherwise never have met. No minutes were taken of what they said to each other when they did meet; otherwise, perhaps, we might have on record an animated conversation between Miss Octavia Hill and Mrs. G. H. Sheppard on the use of the term 'lady' . . . But the organ of the feminist movement, the *Englishwomen's Journal*, which was started in 1858, never missed a chance throughout the years that followed of publishing verbatim reports of the papers given to the Association by all the better-known women members. The *Journal*, indeed, advocated every charitable scheme with equal vigour. An article in 1860 on District Visiting conveyed, by implication, a grim picture: 'Do not be too zealous, do not put the housewife under catechism, do not reproach her with not keeping her cottage cleaner . . .'

But it was with more modern philanthropy that the feminists

were mainly concerned, with serving it up to their reading public without its sauce of sentimentality—and one article in 1864 is typical of many that they published expressing the conviction that

'*the* natural channel for the energies of most women of the upper class is that of helping the poor—I do not mean mere alms-giving or mere district-visiting or mere nursing . . . I include all manner of social authority and supervision, headship of workhouses and hospitals, inspection of female prisons and lunatic asylums. I would lay no limit to the gradually growing capacities of women and I would have them study thoroughly both the actual state of life among the masses and the scientific laws of political economy under which such a population exists.'[8]

While during the '60's enlightenment was thus being generously widespread and the rest of the feminine world was slowly accustoming itself to the idea of this new, very advanced, practical charity, the last important movement within the period—that of housing and planning for the poor—was under way. The living conditions of the poor had for many years been a reformers' topic; Dickens' article on the matter, for instance, in an 1854 number of *Household Words* had caused much uneasiness. In 1860 a long article in the *Englishwomen's Journal*, suggesting means of improving the dwellings of the working classes, indicated that women were turning their minds to larger domestic problems than their own. And in 1864 Octavia Hill's three model houses in Paradise Place* were tenanted. Her attitude from the first was characterised by judicious wisdom; she handled her tenants firmly and insisted on regular payment of rent in return for her services as landlord. 'It is far easier to be helpful than to have patience and self-control sufficient when the time comes for seeing suffering and not relieving it,' observed Octavia ruefully— and refrained from whitewashing her tenants' walls for them. As a faithful child of the Social Science Association she stuck closely to all the new philanthropic by-laws; it was her constant

* The three houses were acquired by Ruskin, who urged that the scheme should be made to pay and that he should receive 5 per cent on his capital so that others might, on finding it profitable, follow Octavia's example and automatically raise the whole standard of working class housing.

endeavour to aid the poor without almsgiving, to raise their sense
of proper self-pride and not to strew bounty on them in the gutter.
Her unsentimental pity and her good business head ensured
success and steady expansion for her housing scheme—and, ten
years later, the feature of personal collection of rents by women
was also incorporated into an even more ambitious project of
Susanna Winkworth's.[9] For she herself chose a suitable plot of
ground for building, succeeded in forming a company to pur-
chase. And, with her intimate knowledge of the life and habits
of the poor—derived in the first place, as was usual for Victorian
women, from that apocalyptic storehouse, the Sunday School—
she was then able to provide convenient and comfortable houses
for them.

There were, in addition to these business-like philanthropists,
many women working by means of purse or pen, outside the
main stream of philanthropy—women like Lady Byron and
Baroness Burdett-Coutts, who played the parts of progressive
Ladies Bountiful, or Harriet Martineau, who resembled rather a
practical Village Queen. Both Lady Byron and Baroness Burdett-
Coutts spent much of their wealth on works of thoughtful, considered charity, but while the former made direct contact with
women social workers, the latter made use of her henchman,
Dickens. As her almoner he investigated the appeals she received
and, having weeded them out, drew her attention to the more
distressing cases. 'Trust me that I will be a faithful steward of
your bounty,' he wrote in 1853—and cast his zestful novelist's
eye over such characters as 'Mr. Burgess—a common begging
letter writer—four post bed-stead in room—admirable steak on
fire—handsome wife—two extraordinarily jovial children—cup-
board full of provender—coals in stock—everything particularly
cheerful and cosy.'[10] Mendacious mendicity did not have much
chance against astute Victorian benevolence.

No such go-between, however, was needed for Harriet Martineau, who advocated organised philanthropy by her pen, and
proceeded to organise her own in her village of Ambleside.[11]
There, as its charitable dictator, she forcibly improved the minds
of her maids; placed her library at the disposal of deserving
villagers; provided the sick with nourishing invalid foods; formed
a building society; and delivered lectures on domestic economy,

ethics of communal housebuilding, politics, hygiene, emigration, history and above all, temperance.* Ambleside, in short, was kept on its toes in a state of constant, charitable tension and may well have cast an occasional harassed glance of envy at the neighbouring village of Rydal which had prudently chosen to give refuge to a poet rather than to a political economist.

The women philanthropists presented strange contrasts as they pursued their works of charity; their individuality unblurred by the community of their interests. The conception of a charitable lady as a vague, elegant figure with a little basket on her arm, no longer squared with the facts and she had to yield place gracefully to more distinctive, if more substantial, forms; to Frances Cobbe, large and imperturbable under her umbrella, picking her way through the puddles of dark, filthy closes on her way to Night School; to Mary Carpenter, with her 'plain care-worn face and angular stooping figure, fixing her light blue eyes on her hearers with the intensity of an amiable Ancient Mariner, who only wanted to talk philanthropy';[12] to Lady Byron, slight and stately—a cool, interested spectator; to Harriet Martineau, indomitably good-humoured and talkative, telescoping her ear-trumpet across the room to collect her villagers' muttered contributions to the discussions she led; to Octavia Hill, that small, composed landlord, collecting her rents punctually in all weathers, from her belligerent tenants . . . Despite their dissimilarity, a certain sturdiness of spirit and practical, sympathetic determination they all had in common—without which no amount of imagination, moral arrogance or kindliness would have been able to carry them through the ardours of philanthropy.

2. FEUDAL QUEEN TO SOCIAL WORKER

This extraordinary increase of interest taken by Victorian

---

* Miss Martineau achieved her greatest success with her lectures on drink, at which she showed coloured prints of the stomach, demonstrating the progress of disease in a drunkard's interior. It is recorded that for 80 minutes she held a 'closely packed audience breathlessly attentive—the only interruption coming from a young man who staggered out and fainted at the door . . .'

women in the living conditions of the poor did not, of course, go
unchronicled by the novelist. Most novelists were prepared to
agree that charitable impulses were becoming to a woman; but
many showed an unworthy reluctance to double the role of
heroine and social worker. Under no consideration would they
consent to clothe their Ideal in a uniform of utility cut—no
matter how many distressed needlewomen had been at its fashion-
ing. Both Dickens, now, and Trollope later, for instance, felt that
usefulness could go too far. The former's own practical benevolence and the very fact of his stewardship of the Baroness Burdett-
Coutts' charity strengthened his belief that good works by women
should be carried out by remote control and never, above all, by
direct participation in committee work of any kind. To what
individuality his heroines had he held grimly and refused to
have them absorbed in 'The Women of England, the Daughters
of Britain, the Sisters of all the Cardinal Virtues, separately, the
Ladies of a Hundred Denominations.'[13] Esther Summerson may
be taken as expressing Dickens' idea of the extent to which
women's charity should stretch in her wish 'to be as useful as I
could, to render what kind services I could to those immediately
around me and to try to let that circle of duty gradually and
naturally expand itself.'

Dickens went further than most writers of the period in condemning organised philanthropy for women, whatever their age.
Even Disraeli, in *Coningsby* (1844), allowed Lady Everingham
to superintend schools and organise societies of relief with well-
bred charm and gaiety. In general, it was only the heroines whom
novelists felt were debarred from active social work by the con-
ventions of youth and innocence; scenes of misery and vice were
not for such as them. And in actual fact, few of the women
philanthropists began their labours before they had reached the
age of thirty. But apart from this question of stamina there was
also the problem of romance; the remote, untouched quality of
a heroine must surely suffer if she were to admit—before marriage—to being an enthusiastic member of such an organisation
as 'The Society for the Diffusion of Sanitary Knowledge' . . .
Kingsley expressed in an illuminating paragraph the rueful uneasiness of all the chivalrous at heart. Women novelists felt less
concern.

Grace curtsied, blushed and shook all over. What could Lord Scoutbush want to say to her?

That indeed was not very easy to discover at first; for Scoutbush
felt so strongly the oddity of taking a pretty young woman into his
counsel on a question of sanitary reform that he felt mightily inclined to laugh.[14]

The tendency, therefore, was to confine the heroine's charity
within the familiar limits of district visiting and teaching while
the other female characters of the novel for whom the author
felt less personal responsibility—the married ladies, clergymen's
widows, affluent spinsters and distant relatives—took over the
more specialised and constructive branches of philanthropy.

The thoughts, doubts and sense of awakening responsibility
that stirred in the feminine world in the period around 1850
were given sympathetic utterance by Kingsley in both *Yeast*
(1848) and *Alton Locke* (1850). In the former he broke new
ground by studying Honoria, not from the standpoint of her
equals, but from that of the poor whom she toiled to help and
whose independence she destroyed by her bounty. Honoria was
young and beautiful but 'a staunch believer in that peculiar creed
which allows everyone to feel for the poor but themselves'—and,
as an equally staunch Christian Socialist, Kingsley had no option
but to condemn her—more in reverence than in wrath, however.

'Miss Honoria is an angel of holiness, herself, Sir; and therefore she
goes on without blushing or suspecting, where our blood would boil
again. She sees people in want, and thinks it must be so, and pities
them and relieves them. But she don't know want herself; and, therefore she don't know that it makes men beasts and devils . . . And
there's another mistake in your charitable great people, sir. When
they see poor folk sick or hungry before their eyes, they pull out
their purses fast enough, God bless them . . . But the oppression . . .
and the want . . . and the filth, and the lying, and the swearing, and
the profligacy and the sickening weight of debt—oh, sir, they never
felt this . . . You can have no knowledge, sir, of the whining, canting
deceit and lies which those poor miserable labourers' wives palm on
charitable ladies. If they weren't angels, some of them, they'd lock up
their purses and never give away another farthing.'

Such an attack upon 'indiscriminate and boundless almsgiving'

unmistakably dates *Yeast* as having been written before the
feminine philanthropic movement had got into its stride—for
such simple largesse as Honoria's was seldom to be found mentioned in the novel once the idea of running the Girls' Friendly
Society had taken root in the minds of novelists as a suitable
activity for a heroine. Kingsley was, however, writing in a transition period, and in *Alton Locke* he provided a useful and
thoughtful study of the development of a woman from feudal
queen to social worker. The two types of philanthropy, which
are sharply contrasted, differ less in their scope than in their
motive-force. Lady Ellerton is first shown as indulging her liberality from a sub-conscious desire to satisfy her husband's conception of her:

A helpmeet, if not an oracle guide for her husband in all these
noble plans, she had already acquainted herself with every woman on
the estate; she was the dispenser not merely of alms . . . but of advice, comfort and encouragement. She not only visited the sick and
taught in the schools . . . but seemed, from the hints which I
gathered, to be utterly devoted, body and soul, to the welfare of the
dwellers on her husband's land.

But Kingsley demanded more of his social workers than this.
On the death of her husband, Lady Ellerton's personal interest
in charity is at an end, and it is not until she has discovered the
happiness of doing good for its own sake, has felt the independent
love of the idea of charity, that she satisfies Kingsley's ideal of
a woman philanthropist. With Fabian lucidity she states her
case:

'The blow came . . . With my idol went from me that sphere of
labour which was to witness the triumph of my pride. I saw the estate
pass into other hands; a mighty change passed over me . . . In
poverty and loneliness I thought out the problems of society and
seemed to myself to have found the one solution—self-sacrifice . . . I
had given largely to every charitable organisation and one by one
every institution disappointed me; they seemed, after all, only means
for keeping the poor in their degradation by making it just not intolerable to them . . . Then I tried association among my own sex—
among the most miserable and degraded of them . . . To become the
teacher, the minister, the slave of those whom I was trying to rescue
was now my one idea; to lead them on, not by machinery but by pre-

cept, by example. And I have succeeded—as others will succeed . . .
amid the great new world of enfranchised and fraternal labour.'

Ten years later, the model philanthropist, although equally
disinterested in her labours, was less vocal and idealistic. For
philanthropy was now an accepted fact in the lives of women,
and, with 640 charitable institutions flourishing throughout the
country in 1862, no novelist need have felt it his duty to promote
even more enthusiasm. There was, however, considerable difference of opinion among writers as to the scope and extent of
charity advisable for their heroines. Charlotte Yonge allowed
hers exactly the same latitude as she herself had been given—in
a High Church family, that had thrived, even in the nursery,
upon foreign missions. Like Charlotte, her heroines taught in
village schools, ran friendly societies, read aloud to the poor. But
although her novels, full of such activities, reflect the steady progress of the philanthropic movement, Kingsley's earlier attack
upon almsgiving is more in harmony with its spirit. Such radical
ideals as his of a changed structure of society, with rich and poor
working together, were quite abhorrent to Miss Yonge. Albinia
Kendal, in *The Young Stepmother* (1861), sought to have slum
houses abolished, and Theodora Martin, in *Heart's Ease* (1854),
was pleased to act as the mentor of the parish—but it was the
intention of neither, by so doing, to indicate dissatisfaction with
the basic state of society; all they wished to do was to ameliorate
—up to a point—living conditions for the lower classes, who,
naturally enough, had not their advantages—and never would
have. In 1865, Miss Yonge went further and poured unsparing
scorn upon misguided, feminist social workers in *The Clever
Woman of the Family*. The Clever Woman is Rachel, to whom
everything is 'a system', whose light reading for the railway
carriage is a report of the Social Science Congress, who writes
articles entitled 'Am I Not a Sister?', who starts an Industrial
School for Lacemakers which comes to an ignominious end, but
who, finally, purged of her advanced ideas, is allowed to relapse
into an ideal wife and mother. In common with Miss Carpenter,
Rachel has the philanthropic eye.

Rachel was eloquent over the crying evils of a system that chained
the laceworkers to an unhealthy occupation in their early childhood

and made an overstocked market and underpaid workers . . . and held Fanny fast to listen by a sort of fascination in her overpowering earnestness and great fixed eyes—which when once their grasp was taken would not release their victim.

There was now visible, in the novel, a certain diffidence in the approach of the heroines to the poor that had not been evident before; their welcome was not always assured, as in former years. As for the practice of tract-distributing—the passage of time had not raised its stock with novelists. Mrs. Norton, for instance, mentioned

Mariana, whose life was spent in those careful charities which a narrow income does not make impossible where there is a willing mind. Steady and unceasing was her attendance on the poor; not flinging tracts and warnings into the cottages but coming to them in sickness and sorrow, patient, gentle and consoling.[15]

Rhoda Broughton's Kate, too, felt the futility of such charity:

Kate had intended to sow the tracts broadcast but now she had not the heart to offer one. How absurd it seemed to offer food for the mind as a substitute for that bodily food which was evidently so sorely wanted.[16]

It was obvious that never far from the minds of novelists was hovering the dark Pardiggle spectre. The philanthropic movement was too powerful to be seriously jolted by Dickens' caricature, in *Bleak House* (1853), of a strong-minded social worker, 'a formidable style of lady with spectacles, a prominent nose and a loud voice', but nevertheless protests against the conception echoed at intervals in the novel down the next twenty years. The doom of tracts in all their sanctimony had been pronounced, no matter how many assurances were given of their popularity. In 1866 a writer in the *Englishwomen's Journal* was still stoutly asserting that although she 'entered upon the duty of tract distributing with great distaste, although there seemed to be an assumption of superiority in it and we had an objection to tracts themselves—they were gratefully received.' But it must have been impossible for any novelist to contemplate a reference to tract-distribution without hearing a distant growl of

'Have I read the little book wot you left? No, I an't read the little book wot you left. There ant nobody here as knows how to read it and if there wos it wouldn't be suitable to me. It's a book fit for a babby and I'm not a babby.'[17]

It was Mrs. Pardiggle and not Mrs. Jellyby who did the mischief; foreign missions had a far smaller public than all the everyday* charities at which Dickens struck out. And when he satirised the former lady's rapacious benevolence he set against her no companion picture of the charitable worker whom he admitted did exist—one who 'did a great deal and made no noise at all'. In consequence, there was a very understandable eagerness on the part of later novelists to stress the essentially sympathetic and feminine approach of their heroines. One young lady, indeed, came out into the open with: 'Bertie, I see you think me one of the Pardiggle class—more anxious to put myself forward than that good should be done.'[18] So that a certain ladylike languor in the heroines' good offices may safely be attributed to writers preferring to soft-pedal their charitable impulses than to allow a suspicion of officiousness to cloud their fame.

The uses of philanthropy to the novelist, however, were many. It had appeared before—and still occasionally did appear—as a last resort for a broken-spirited woman after life had done its worst to her. In *Not Wisely But Too Well*, Rhoda Broughton took full use of its medicinal properties. When her heroine's heart received its first bruise she was given a short but salutary course in good works; and when it was irrevocably broken she was consigned to a band of 'holy devoted women, dedicated to charitable work' until her youth was absorbed in 'a grey, beautiless, middle-age'. Miss Broughton was candid and unashamed in her exploitation of philanthropy; Mrs. Lynn Linton treated it with rather more respect in stressing its ability to make empty lives purposeful, and exclusively domestic lives more interesting. In *Sowing the Wind* (1867), the problem arises which the philanthropically-minded wife must often have had to face. The

---

* Like Johnson, who could find no point of precedency between a louse and a flea, Dickens was incapable of picking out one charitable activity as being less objectionable than another. He impatiently dismissed them all. 'I am a School Lady, I am a Visiting Lady. I am a Reading Lady. I am a Distributing Lady . . .'

heroine, Isola, is torn between her duty of obedience to her husband and her desire to do charitable work outside her home:

'What can I do?' asked Isola, with a kind of despair in her voice.

'Do? are there no poor to help?—no charities to see to? Have you no duties do you think? Was it ever meant that you should lead a life of nothing but lazy self-indulgence while there is all this misery and wretchedness in the world to try to cure? . . .'

'But what can I do, Jane?' returned Isola. 'I should like to visit the poor and go to Sunday schools and hospitals but how can I when so distinctly against my husband's wishes?'

It was hard indeed for the Victorian maiden, within her red-brick neo-Gothic refuge, who heard the call of philanthropy— and was not allowed to lay down her embroidered fire-screen and respond to the summons . . . Isola was held back by her obligations to her husband, who was jealous of outside interests. Another heroine was frustrated by a sense of duty to her parents who considered her too young. It might be difficult for us fully to appreciate the mastery over women's minds that the idea of charitable work—as a good in itself—had assumed, had we not such documentary evidence available as this minor novel of 1862, *A Maiden of our Own Day*. Let it first be stated that the author, Miss Florence Wilford, did not think it necessary to explain her heroine, Gyneth, in any way; she pleaded no abnormalcy; no extenuating Evangelicalism; no unhappy home circumstances. She would have us believe that Gyneth is (as, indeed, the title indicates) a normal, contented, moderately high-church, Victorian young woman. As such, then, the animating desire of her life is to take part in philanthropic activities. Her nights are haunted by District Visitors; her waking dreams by Ragged Children. But her parents, though not unsympathetic, consider the responsibilities too great for one so young.

'I honour your motives,' said her father. 'You make me feel self-reproachful for the selfishness of my own youth when I took hardly any concern about the welfare of my fellow-creatures. If I refuse to let you join in district visiting and so on it is not because I do not approve your desire to be useful; cherish that desire and in some years' time you may be all that you now dream of.'

With a mighty effort, Gyneth resolves to obey her parents and to exercise her charity nearer home, in less spectacular ways. But as charity is the ruling spirit of the town in which she lives 'the daily course of her life seemed so frivolous that to look forward to a continuance of it was a positive pain' and the superiority of the Rector's daughter, who, although two years younger than Gyneth, has her District Working Society and Sunday School class upon which to wreak her benevolence, becomes very hard to bear:

'As you are so very anxious to be of use, Miss Deshon, why don't you ask papa to give you a district?' said Augusta patronisingly. 'I know he is in want of some lady visitors now for there are one or two particularly *good* districts vacant—such as a lady *can* go to.'
'I think I would rather have a particularly *bad* one if I were a visitor' said Gyneth impulsively.

In the meantime, however, Gyneth's existence has been less of a positive pain than she feared; there have been compensations . . . And as the day of her marriage approaches and the flame of her philanthropy, though untended, is found to be still flickering brightly, we are allowed a glimpse of the blissful prospect opening before her—of labouring in a 'famous preserve of ragged children' near her husband's London house. With maidenhood safely behind her, there is no end to the philanthropy a young matron may indulge in.

As *Middlemarch* (1871) is set some forty years earlier,* Dorothea Brooke's charitable urges have to take a somewhat different form. The idea of almsgiving and village charity has little appeal for Dorothea and is dismissed by George Eliot in a sentence, where Kingsley had to employ a novel:

What could she do?—what ought she to do? . . . With some endowment of stupidity and conceit, she might have thought that a

* Many of the best-known Victorian novels e.g. *Shirley*, *The Mill on the Floss, Vanity Fair, Wives and Daughters* amongst others, are set in earlier periods than the date of writing; so that often, while the thoughts and sentiments are unmistakably Victorian the social conditions are those of another age. As far as possible I have, in each case, attempted to keep the distinction clear.

Christian young lady of fortune should find her ideal of life in village
charities, patronage of the humbler clergy, the perusal of 'Female
Scripture Characters' . . . and the care of her soul over her embroidery in her own boudoir.

But although Dorothea felt uncertainty about the ways in
which she could do good—'building good cottages—there could
be no doubt about that'—and she applied herself to her plans
for rebuilding the dilapidated cottages on Mr. Brooke's and Sir
James's estates, with all the singlemindedness of a reformer: 'I
used to come from the village with all that dirt and coarse ugli-
ness like a pain with me . . . I think we have no right to come
forward and urge wider changes for good until we have tried to
alter the evils which lie under our own hands.'

With her enthusiastic vision, practical interest in housing, a
head for plans and a pencil ready to draw them, Dorothea is
ahead of her times. But in at least one important respect she is
true to her 1831 milieu. To put her plans into effect she is dependent upon the goodwill of masculine henchmen.

And yet, despite Dorothea, the novelists' attitude towards
philanthropy in any other female character than the heroine is
at once freer and less self-conscious. With women over a certain
age—or with married women—they felt more at ease and, consequently, in them we see less distorted reflections of the new
type of woman to whom philanthropy had given birth. Mary
Boyd, for example, an ideal social worker whom Gyneth strove
to emulate in *A Maiden of our Own Day*, bore, in her work at
least, a definite resemblance to Mary Carpenter. She was a spinster, untiring in her work among the poor, visiting in one of
the worst districts of the town and running Sunday School classes.
She was of independent means which she used to found two industrial schools—one for girls and one for boys—the former
being particularly under her own care as 'Red Lodge' was under
Miss Carpenter's. Her appearance was unremarkable except for
the 'cool clear kindliness of her face' and she gave an impression
of unsparing and sympathetic efficiency. Such was Miss Boyd,
Social Worker, the answer to Gyneth's maiden prayers. Charity
was no longer an affair of heroics but of hard work and Gyneth,
taken upon a tour of Miss Boyd's Industrial Home, confined her
prosaic raptures over it to the orderly arrangements of kitchen,

3

laundry, dining-room—to her idol's competence rather than to her sacrificial spirit. For the latter quality she was conscious of possessing herself. What was really important was to put it to methodical use; to have a System.* The efficiency was all.

As philanthropy becomes more and more a common-place of life we find, scattered throughout the novels from 1860 onwards, frequent references to such contemporary charitable organisations as Night Schools and Ragged Schools; not all writers felt it necessary to take up the cudgels for or against. Those, however, who came into direct contact with women social workers bore the mark henceforward. George MacDonald never quite got over the effect of his friendship with Lady Byron; and in *The Vicar's Daughter* (1872), which he dedicated to her, he gave a double dose of charity. First comes a recognisable, if idealised, portrait of Lady Byron.

> Lady Bernard was slight and appeared taller than she was, being rather stately than graceful with a commanding forehead and still blue eyes. She gave at first the impression of coldness with a touch of haughtiness. But this was, I think, chiefly the result of her inherited physique. Never did woman of rank step more triumphantly over the barriers which the cumulated custom of ages has built between the classes of society . . . If ever there was a woman who lived the outer life for the sake of others it was she . . . I believe no one knew half the munificent things she did or what an immense proportion of her large income she spent on other people. But as she said herself, no one understood the worth of money better: and no one liked better to have the worth of it: therefore she always administered her charity with some view to the value of the probable return—with some regard, that is, to the amount of good likely to result to others from aid given.

But MacDonald had a better grasp of the basic principles of the new philanthropy than to confine himself to eulogies upon Lady Bernard's good business head; in the same novel, as a contrast to the rich philanthropist, he presents an active worker among the poor, Marion Clare. Neither Lady Bernard nor Marion Clare is the Vicar's daughter—the author's charity does

---

* It was not enough, in fact, to adopt the attitude of one of Mrs. Linton's characters, who said, cheerfully, 'I am fond of the poor—are you?'

not go as far as that. It is enough for his heroine to look on with
wide, admiring eyes at the feats of strong-minded women. But
Miss Clare is young, attractive and All But a Heroine. She lives
in a poverty-stricken neighbourhood, acts as arbitrator and friend
to her neighbours and seeks, by her example, to raise their self-
respect. Much of the character is taken from Octavia Hill—not
only in the general outline of her social work is there a resemblance but in traits of character and details of organisation. Miss
Clare, for instance, shares Miss Hill's whitewashing proclivities.
Her efficiency, however, does not stand in the way of her being
wooed throughout the novel and the resolution of her romance
is made its culminating issue. For her heart is so much in her
District that to leave either behind her is out of the question; and
yet to rear a family in squalid surroundings is equally undesir-
able . . . It is at this impasse that the nexus between rich
philanthropist and social worker has its modest triumph. Lady
Bernard's intervention provides, not only the nuptial solution,
but a housing scheme on Octavia Hill lines.

The result of Lady Bernard's cogitation is, in so far, to be seen in
the rapid rise of a block of houses at no great distance from London
on the N.W. railway, planned under the instructions of Marion Clare.
The design of them is to provide accommodation for all Marion's
friends with room to add largely to their number. Lady Bernard has
also secured ground sufficient for great extension of the present building should it prove desirable . . . Marion has undertaken to collect
the rents and believes that she will thus, in time, gain an additional
hold of the people for their good although the plan may at first
expose her to misunderstanding. From thorough calculation she is
satisfied she can pay Lady Bernard 5 per cent. for her money, lay out
all that is necessary for keeping the property in thorough repair and
accumulate a fund besides to be spent on building more houses should
her expectations of these be answered. In the centre of the building is
a house for herself where she will have her own private advantage in
the inclusion of a large space, primarily for the entertainment of her
friends.

We need go no further. With this sober suggestion of a model
housing scheme to provide a home for Social Worker and District
alike we have reached a point where, on looking back, indiscriminate bounty has faded into unreality. In thirty years philan-

thropy had travelled far. Exactly how far can best be indicated by substituting for Marion Clare, Disraeli's Lady Everingham or even Kingsley's Honoria. And in the pleasing contemplation of a feudal queen coping with rents, five per cents and truculent tenants we shall comprehend how organic a change the earlier ideal of charitable womanhood had undergone.

CHAPTER II

That Noble Body of Governesses

1. A VICTORIAN INSTITUTION

THE Victorian Governess, as distinctive a feature of her age as the antimacassar, family album or 'Christian Year', played a part in the national life whose importance and complexity should not be underestimated. In her time she not only filled, with equal ladylike resignation, the anomalous roles of household drudge and novel heroine, but also incurred a certain uneasy degree of responsibility for the birth of the Girton Girl. Her own emergence as a Victorian institution can be attributed to various causes.

The bank failures of the thirties had rendered many families destitute and a large number of gently-bred young women, with few qualifications other than drawing-room accomplishments, were forced to seek employment. At the same time, the demand for governesses was steadily increasing. In the Georgian era, daughters had, in the main, been allowed to pick up a haphazard education from their parents or brothers' tutor. The alternatives were fashionable, expensive boarding-schools or governesses— but the latter were by no means numerous. With the rise of the wealthy middle classes, however, and the growing stress on the sanctity of family life, a new situation developed.

Parents, rich enough to have pretensions for their daughters, were often incapable of educating them themselves; an excess of respectability and prudery forbade masculine intervention; more and more accomplishments were becoming necessary for a young lady to find a bidder in the marriage market. A distressed gentlewoman in the home to educate and refine their offspring seemed the natural, the fitting solution—more especially as there chanced to be such a providential number of distressed gentlewomen at large, pathetically eager to accept any salary, to tolerate any indignity. The issue of this marriage of supply and demand was a new type of broken-spirited, submissive dependent—the Victorian Governess.

To do the Victorians justice, it was not long before her plight touched the heart of all who did not employ her. In 1841, a Governesses' Benevolent Institution was formed to give annuities and to 'afford assistance privately and delicately to ladies in temporary distress'. The Institution was inundated with appeals from destitute governesses—appeals, so heart-breaking and numerous, that the Christian Socialists, under F. D. Maurice, turned their thoughts towards improving the governess' position by more radical methods, by raising the standard of their education so that they would be in a position to command higher salaries.

With the co-operation of Charles Kingsley, a series of Lectures to Ladies was begun in London in 1847, and a committee of professors from King's College was formed to grant certificates of proficiency. The lectures proved an immediate success, and so many women thronged to them in the first year that, in 1848, Queen's College for Women was founded, and in 1849, Bedford College, with a mixed board of Directors. The aims of the colleges, to impart 'female knowledge', were modest and vague but, as a large percentage of the women who attended the classes were ignorant even of the rudiments of grammar and arithmetic, the fine distinction drawn between the higher branches of male and female knowledge did not then worry them unduly. Although most of the women were drawn from the governess or teacher ranks and were there to be taught how to teach, there were others, like George Eliot, who were quite disinterested in their search for knowledge.

If then the Governess, almost despite herself, laid the foundation stone of higher education for women, it was left to others of more resolute, workmanlike spirit to complete the structure. Some women emerged from their course of lectures with grim determination to improve their status as teachers and to raise the standard of feminine education; others, with their former attitude of weary submission to their fate. The latter remained governesses to the end; the former, with whom are associated such names as Miss Beale, Miss Buss, Miss Davies and Mme. Bodichon, set their energies to the double task of improving the education of girls by establishing reliable schools and of rendering their instructors more worthy of their responsibilities by besieging the citadel of university education. But, although from 1848 the course of women's education could be seen to diverge into two distinct channels, the more progressive women by no means left the governesses to struggle on alone. When, in 1858, they set up the Association for the Promotion of the Employment of Women, their utmost efforts were directed not only towards finding situations for unemployed governesses but also towards persuading them to try other types of occupation. Here, however, the few remnants of pride, which governesses still clutched desperately around them, proved as effective as chain-mail in obstructing the penetration of new ideas. For they felt that, as governesses, however wretched and underpaid, they were known to be ladies: if they descended to any other occupation it might be thought that they had been trained to earn their living, not forced to do so by cruel circumstances.

The influence of the governess, then, upon the novels of the period falls into quite a different category from that of the effect of the feminist educational movement of the '50s and '60's. Her continual appearance in the novel tends to blur the issue, and it is only when the novel is released from its governess-trammels that it is possible to judge how far the Victorian novelist's ideal of womanhood was affected by the more advanced ideas on education and careers for women.

It is easy to understand the popularity of the governess with the Victorian novelist. In 1851 there were no fewer than 24,770 governesses in England, and in point of pathos even distressed needlewomen had to yield place to indigent governesses. An allusion to a governess in a novel was as sure to arouse a stock, emotional response in the minds of the readers as a reference to death. Everyone was familiar with her conventional attributes. She was bound to be a lady—preferably the daughter of a clergyman; she was always impoverished, unprotected, and, by virtue of her circumstances, reasonably intelligent and submissive. But though she appeared on the scene in this ready-made gown, there was nothing to prevent the novelist embellishing it to his taste, adding a flounce of coquettishness here or a slashing of deceitfulness there. In addition, because her tenure of what was usually a disagreeable post was involuntary, she was absolved from any suspicion of strong-mindedness in earning her living and thus was especially dear to the reactionary novelist.

It may be well to sketch in the everyday background of the governess from contemporary evidence before considering her through the novelists' eyes. For although it is indisputable that her position was not only hard, but at times inhumanly cruel, it is equally true that there must have been some governesses who were not dissatisfied with their posts. Lady Stanley, in a letter to her daughter-in-law, Henrietta, in 1843, gives the employer's point of view:

'It does seem wonderful that good or even tolerable governesses should be so scarce and that their expectations should be so exorbitant in times when one might suppose that many would wish for a governess who cannot afford to pay them high and that very many well-educated women must be wanting bread. I am much afraid that you will not get *all* you require under a £100—but certainly my own opinion is that so very few governesses are capable of *teaching everything* that I should prefer a humble professor at £80 and spend the remaining £20 on masters. They are sufficiently well grounded in German to be able to go on with the language—Musick is the only thing a governess ought to know enough of to keep them well up in their practising but I must say I do not think they have musical bumps.'[1]

The salary Lady Stanley mentions—£100—was the maximum a governess could expect and one which she very rarely obtained. It was, indeed, one which very few employers could afford to pay. Thackeray, in 1850, mentions that his children's governess, Miss Trulock, 'has had a good offer of £100 a year and I'm afraid must leave us'. Thirty or forty guineas a year was an average salary for a governess, although Miss Parkes, in a paper to the Social Science Congress in 1862, revealed that she had had no fewer than 810 applicants for a post which carried with it a salary of only £15 per annum.

The founding of Queen's College in 1848 was greeted, on the whole, with approval. Richard Cobbold, whose sympathies were far from feminist, struck a note of rhetorical enthusiasm in the lecture he delivered in the same year on behalf of the Governesses' Benevolent Institution.

'At this period when it is proposed to give retiring pensions to national schoolmistresses, shall that noble body of governesses whose higher attainments and qualifications adorn our family circle be excluded from the sympathy and support of the families of this great kingdom? Forbid it, O ye great and powerful!'

Then, swiftly descending to practical measures, he advocated 'exalting the tone of Female Education throughout the country by the establishment of a Queen's College in London whence certificates of qualification may be obtained'[2] and providing a home for governesses between engagements, with temporary assistance for deserving cases, an Annuity Fund, a Provident Fund and Asylum for the Aged.

A more doubtful attitude was adopted by Lady Eastlake in the *Quarterly Review*, in 1848, in her celebrated article on *Vanity Fair, Jane Eyre* and the Governesses' Benevolent Institution. She was disturbed by the project of founding Queen's College for 'as the real and highest responsibility and recommendation of an *English* governess must ever rest more upon her moral than her literary qualifications, the plan of subjecting her to an examination upon the latter appears to us neither wise nor fair'. She went on, severely, to give an interesting sidelight upon the new recruits to the governess ranks.

'The case of the governess is so much the harder than that of any other class . . . a being our equal in birth, manners and education but our inferior in worldly wealth . . . There is no other class which so cruelly requires its members to be in birth, mind and manners above their station, in order to fit them for their station . . .' But— 'Farmers and tradespeople are now educating their daughters for governesses as a mode of advancing them a step in life, and thus a number of underbred young women have crept into the profession who have brought down the salaries and interfered with the rights of those whose birth and misfortunes leave them no other refuge.'

The full effect of the 'Lectures to Ladies' upon the governess' outlook is mirrored in an Independent, Christian, Non-Sectarian periodical which made its first appearance in 1854. The *Governess* or *A Repertory of Female Education* aimed at being 'a medium through which friends of Education might communicate their ideas and stimulate each other in the good cause'. The

Repertory is a somewhat pathetic mixture of old and new ideas. Notes of Queen's College lectures, articles on Froebel methods and callisthenics' diagrams mingle uneasily with sentimental extracts and fancy needlework patterns. The influence of Mr. Maurice on the minds of the editorial staff of the *Repertory* was strong however and, taking as its watchword 'Elevate the governess in the scale of society and you elevate society itself', it expressed its opinion freely on several important points. It condemned female education generally as 'limited in extent, meagre in quality and inadequate to the future necessities of the rising generation', deprecated the time spent in the schoolroom in the acquisition of accomplishments and explained the difficulties of the governess as 'arising principally from her own imperfect education and the want of educational knowledge in the parents of her pupils'. But having gone so far, the *Repertory* knew where to stop in its advocacy of a liberal education for ladies. 'We have no intention of following the American example and having ladies graduate as physicians for instance—we have no such absurd cravings. By marking out clearly the specific work for which women are by their natures adapted a safeguard will be erected against the growth of restless aspirations.'

Such was the attitude of mind that made the feminists at times despair of ever improving the lot of the governesses, as they sat, perched in ladylike indecision, on the fence. One number of their periodical, alone, reveals their divided loyalties, when an article condemning useless accomplishments is followed, in the correspondence columns, by an animated interchange of letters on the modelling of wax-flowers. The correspondence is worth lingering over as a disclosure of the importance of 'extras' in a 'liberal education' in 1855; extras acquired, it seems, even at great personal risk.

'Sir,
My daughter who is receiving a liberal education with a view of becoming a teacher, if necessary, has a great fancy for wax modelling. My only objection to her learning it is the deleterious nature of the colouring matter of the wax . . . the poison of which is absorbed into the pores of the hand and causes paralysis sometimes to an alarming degree . . .'

Next month, however, considerable space was devoted to a reassuring reply:

Sir,

I have modelled many wax flowers during the last few years and have felt no ill effects from the wax which is prepared by Mrs. Peachey, 35, Rathbone Place. As she devotes her *whole* time to the art and is herself in good health though she has modelled wax flowers for years I think her testimony worthy of credit . . . Should this information be satisfactory to your correspondent I should be pleased as it is a pity that her daughter should be deprived of so delightful a recreation.'

Higher education was raising new problems for the governess and the correspondence columns of the *Repertory* reveal the unsettled state of her mind. A pathetic letter from 'A Governess who wishes to learn Latin' enclosed a lengthy quotation from Bulwer to the effect that clever men prefer mediocre wives—and asked if this were indeed the case. A question to which the Editor diplomatically returned no answer. For the time had not yet come for learning to be acknowledged as a good in itself, without any reference to its possible effect upon marriage prospects. Lectures to Ladies, Latin, wax-flowers—all these were only in the nature of temporary opiates to deaden the senses of the governess to the misery of her situation. She was still firm in her conviction that her only true escape, her one hope of happiness on earth, lay in matrimony.

2. BEFORE 1848

The governess made her first real début in the literature of the Victorian age in *The Governess* by Lady Blessington—a novel written by the fashionable authoress in crusading spirit, to hoist aloft the banner of a class she considered peculiarly oppressed. In November, 1839, she wrote to her niece:

'I am very much gratified by what you tell me of Miss Lane's approbation of *The Governess*. It was my anxious wish to point attention and excite sympathy towards a class from which more is expected and to whom less is accorded, than to any other. It has always struck me that no situation is so painful as that of a Gentle-

woman constantly occupied in the difficult task of forming the youthful minds, and instilling not only all the rudiments of education, but
what is of infinitely more importance, those principles on which the
happiness here and hereafter, of her pupils must depend; and exposed
to the neglect, rudeness or jealousies of those who confide to her the
most sacred of all trusts, the minds of their children.'[3]

The pattern of *The Governess* was one which became, in its
broad outlines, more and more familiar in succeeding novels.
The beautiful young heroine, Clara Mordaunt, is left destitute
by the bankruptcy and suicide of her father and is forced to seek
a post as a governess. In the four situations she fills before she is
rescued by an offer of marriage from a lord and a legacy from a
relative, she experiences all the miseries peculiar to the governess' lot. She is distrusted by the servants, despised by her
upstart employers, made unhappy by her uncouth charges.
She has to share an attic bedroom with the children, to sit
unheeded at the dinner-table, to tolerate the rude familiari-
ties of the male guests, to submit to drudgery—in exchange for
a salary of 25 guineas a year. The advertisement she answered
gives some idea of the qualifications required of a governess
in 1839.

'She must be of a prepossessing appearance, of refined manners and
a perfect musician. She is required to instruct her pupils in French,
Italian and English; geography and the use of the globes, with music,
drawing and dancing; in all which branches of education she is expected to be a proficient. Equanimity of temper and cheerfulness of
disposition joined to uninterrupted health are indispensable requi-
sites. She must understand cutting out and making children's
dresses.'

In the same year Harriet Martineau's *Deerbrook* was published. The sombre, solitary governess in this novel, Maria
Young, has as little in common with Clara Mordaunt as her
creator with the glittering Lady Blessington. Maria is not young
enough to fill the heroine's role nor sufficiently ill-treated to be
pathetic. She is merely poor, lame, unwell, and independent
enough to find a substitute for love and affection in her thoughts,
her books and her plain sewing. We are constantly catching a
glimpse of such solitary, uncomplaining figures in the back-

ground of the novels of the period and although, in all probability, they give a more representative idea of the governess than the martyred heroines, they have seldom much appeal for either author or reader. The day of the strong-minded woman was surely approaching but Maria Young was some years in advance of her times. She was not only strong-minded but also 'superior', 'philosophical', 'sensible' and 'learned'. Only a novelist of Miss Martineau's impenetrable calibre could have expected the governess to continue to charm her readers after the application of such epithets.

'Strong-minded' was, however, an adjective of infinite elasticity. Maria Young forms an interesting contrast with a later governess, in *Very Successful* (1856), a novel by Bulwer's wife. Rosina Bulwer persists, on every possible occasion, in describing her heroine, a widow of thirty-nine, as a 'strong-minded woman' —although she is allowed in the end to be in sufficient need of a prop to enter into marriage with an aristocratic curate of twenty-eight. The governess convention allowed authors plenty of scope to ride their favourite hobby-horses, and it is therefore the privilege of Rosina's strong-minded widow to rail against the injustice of the marriage laws and the perfidy of men. Much that is characteristic of the author's peculiar cast of mind is often revealed by study of a stock character like that of the governess —for just as Maria Young would confirm every suspicion of Harriet Martineau's mental sturdiness so would Mrs. Pemble give fairly reliable evidence of Rosina's emotional instability.

Dickens' Miss Pinch (1843) was well in the down-trodden tradition, but in 1844 Elizabeth Sewell produced a governess in *Amy Herbert* who acted as a model for many later novel heroines. This moral, high-church tale of the instruction of a small girl by wise parents and a ladylike governess had considerable popularity —mainly, according to a cynical publisher in *Lewis Arundel* (1852), owing to the character of Miss Emily Morton.

'Clever book, Amy Herbert, very. So much tenderness in it, ma'am, nothing pays better than judicious tenderness. The mothers of England like it—the little girls of England like it—and so the husbands of England are forced to pay for it. If you recollect, ma'am, there's a pathetic governess in "Amy Herbert" who calls the children "dearest"; well-imagined character that. She's sold many copies that governess.'[4]

Miss Morton was indeed a paragon—beautiful, shy, religious, high-principled, gentle. But a paragon, it seemed, destined to end her days as a governess in the sunshine of the Herbert family. There is no murmur of possible marriage or change of occupation for Miss Morton. A governess-post, in the rare eventuality of its being comfortable, was obviously considered bliss enough. Such compulsory identification of her interests with those of her employers had, by the year 1848, placed the governess on the level of a superior slave.

The year of revolutions is marked in red in the history of the governess. With the founding of Queen's College and the recent publication of *Vanity Fair* and *Jane Eyre*, she found herself right at the front of the social and literary scene. Two such governesses as Becky and Jane had never before been contemplated. As, hand-in-hand, they took their curtains and listened with shameless composure to the mingled cheers and hisses, they gave an uncomfortable jolt to all previous ideas of governesses. Both possessed to the full the new spirit of independence that the educationists were trying to foster in women of that profession, but, in their case, the spirit came, not through knowledge, but rather from a proper appreciation of their own value as individual human beings.

Jane and Becky had a far more important point in common than that they followed the fashion, set a hundred years earlier, of marrying into their employers' family. They themselves set a new fashion—of considering themselves as women, first, and dependants, second. They were women, earning their livings as governesses, but not knuckling under to circumstances or allowing their personalities to be submerged. Purely literary considerations apart, *Jane Eyre* was of the two the more revolutionary document, the Magna Charta of governesses—and it is as such that Lady Eastlake condemned it in the *Quarterly Review* of 1848.

It is not difficult to see why she should have preferred Becky to Jane and considered her less dangerous, less likely to inculcate levelling doctrines. For, when all is said, Becky's heartlessness and polished villainy were quite apart from her early profession. The evil lessons that could be learned by a governess from Becky were only two—to scamp her duties and to set her cap at her master's son:

> With the young people, whose applause she thoroughly gained, her method was pretty simple. She did not pester their young brains with too much learning, but on the contrary let them have their own way in regard to educating themselves, for what instruction is more effectual than self instruction?[5]

So that though Becky read French romances with Miss Rose, allowed Miss Violet to run wild among the stablemen, took an intelligent interest in Mr. Crawley's pamphlet on Malt, played backgammon with Sir Pitt and, in her spare moments, made a conquest of Rawdon, her evil influence upon the vast reading public of governesses was considered to be in no way comparable to that of the conscientious Jane.

What then, was Jane's especial crime?—One of a tribe of governesses whose especial heritage was submission, she yet indulged herself in passions, emotions and resentments that were the privileges of the upper classes. Because Jane brooded over her unhappy childhood, resented patronage, enjoyed independence, laughed at her betters, fell in love with her master, listened tolerantly to Rochester's immoral history, vanquished her beautiful rival, held on to her integrity, with proud consciousness of her own value to herself, the novel was described as a danger 'to the class of ladies whose cause it affects to advocate'. Lady Eastlake spoke, solemnly, from the depths of her Tory heart:

> 'Altogether the autobiography of Jane Eyre is pre-eminently an anti-Christian composition. There is throughout it a murmuring against the comforts of the rich and against the privations of the poor, which, as far as each individual is concerned, is a murmuring against God's appointment . . . There is that pervading tone of ungodly discontent which is at once the most prominent and the most subtle evil which the law and the pulpit, which all civilised society in fact has at the present day to contend with. We do not hesitate to say that the tone of mind and thought which has overthrown authority abroad and fostered Chartism and rebellion at home, is the same which has also written *Jane Eyre*.'[6]

Although *Jane Eyre* and *Agnes Grey* are contemporary publications they do not approach the governess-question in the same spirit. The latter, though a document of personal experience and suffering, looks back to Lady Blessington's *The Governess*; the former owes no allegiance to the convention of the past and is itself the first of a new type of governess-novel. While *Agnes Grey* is written in a mood of resentful resignation, *Jane Eyre* is composed in one of rebellious independence. The utmost hardship that Jane has to suffer once she becomes a governess is Miss Ingram's scorn, whereas Agnes' petty persecutions and physical hardships are manifold. But Charlotte was not fighting for better living conditions for the governess but for recognition of her equality in spirit, mind and soul. In short, Agnes Grey's problems were such as might well have been dealt with by the Governesses' Benevolent Institution; Jane Eyre's could only be resolved in the hearts and conscience of the nation.

One further characteristic was shared by those three governess heroines—Becky, Agnes and Jane—which is of some interest in view of the fact that till then it had been a convention for novelists to ascribe much of the misery suffered by their governesses to their beauty. The jealousy aroused by Miss Clara Mordaunt's good looks had been the principal reason for her leaving four posts in as many weeks and even the impeccable Miss Emily Morton found her appealing features a disadvantage at times. But neither Thackeray nor the Brontës sued for sympathy for their heroines on that account. Becky was pale and sandy-haired; Jane was small and plain; and as for Agnes—

'I was somewhat dismayed at my appearance on looking in the glass . . . the cold wind had swelled and reddened my hands, uncurled and entangled my hair, and dyed my face of a pale purple; add to this my collar was horribly crumpled, my frock splashed with mud, my feet clad in stout new boots . . .'[7]

Miss Elizabeth Bennet may have had muddy petticoats but she certainly never owned to a pale purple face and such a description as this heavily underlines Lady Eastlake's caustic remark that it seemed to be becoming now the fashion for novelists 'to give no encouragement to the insolence of mere beauty'.

3. THE HEROINE GOVERNESS

Although in the ensuing quarter of a century the position of
the governess gradually improved, the mere fact that she remained a governess militated against any very remarkable
developments in the novelists' conception of her. 1848 was as
memorable a year for the educational feminists as for the governesses, but they did not stop there. For them—for the women
who did—the years that followed showed steady progress from
one well-defined landmark to another, towards their disinterested
ideal of educated womanhood. For those who continued in their
dependent positions as governesses, the Lectures to Ladies and
Queen's College remained the high-water mark in their history.
For although the efforts of the feminists on their behalf undoubtedly led to a new attitude of consideration and there is
little trace in the novel of the sixties of the persecuted martyr,
their position on the whole was so static that it is small wonder
that many novelists gave way to plagiarism and merely modelled
their governesses on the pre-1848 *Amy Herbert* tradition or
produced faithful copies of Miss Becky Sharp or Miss Jane Eyre.
The governess heroines that defy such crude classification between the years 1848 and 1873 are few in number but it is from
such few as there are that an idea can be gained of the uneasy
fluctuations of the later social position of the governess.

The three main types, however, predominated. Of the
daughters of Miss Sharp, Wilkie Collins' Miss Gwilt, in *Armadale*, bears the closest family resemblance. Beautiful, a-moral and
ambitious, she starts out on her career of villainy with deter·
mined purpose. Unlike Becky, who had to be her own mother,
she has a woman-confidante to give her support and encouragement. 'A woman, my dear Lydia, with your appearance, your
manners, your ability and your education, can make almost any
excursions into society that she pleases if only she has money
in her pocket and a respectable reference to appeal to in cases
of emergency.'[8] And, also unlike Miss Sharp, who survives
Thackeray's delicate insinuations about her responsibility for
Jos's death to busy herself on behalf of the 'destitute Orange
Girl, the Neglected Washerwoman' in Bath, Miss Gwilt, dis-

covered in an act of attempted murder, brings her life to a dramatic end. The sensation novel admitted of no nuances.

While Thackeray's imitators were concentrating on villainy, Miss Brontë's followers were equally engrossed in principle and passion. Jane's declaration of her love to Rochester had much to account for; of the governesses who succeeded her it could scarcely be said that they never spoke their love. They might prefix their confessions with such deprecating remarks as 'Perhaps my conduct may be unmaidenly and bold—I cannot help it . . .' But they were not afraid to make their feelings clear and were as ready as Jane to admit any man master, whom they considered worthy of gaining their love. The stress in such novels is on the importance, not of external knowledge, but of inner powers of self-discipline and of spiritual resources. The possession of a mind is not, however, without its appeal, as can be seen from a conversation in Mrs. Betham-Edwards' *The White House by the Sea*, between the heroine, Chatty, and the family doctor.

'You have the stuff in you to make a MAN!—and very rare material that is nowadays; in the first place you have got brains—your perceptive powers are quick, active and correct; in the next place you have got a mind—all the experiences, reflections and conclusions that you have harvested up are of use to you. You can perceive, but what is a far rarer faculty you can reason. On my word, Miss Warne, you surprise me—your education . . .'
'I have none, Sir.'
'Pardon me,' resumed the physician tartly, 'you have had the very best education for you have been self-taught.'[9]

From a review in 1858 of *Riverston* and *The White House by the Sea* it can be inferred that, if the novel-reading public could not have too much of the good thing that was Jane, the reviewers were becoming a little restive:

Those novels introduce us to two governesses who are the daughters direct of Miss Jane Eyre. The governess in an autobiographical novel is pretty sure to be the heroine and authoress thereof. She is the family dissector, the social anatomist; she is a manager of women and of men . . . Of these heroine governesses one can only wish that England may have more of them and the circulating libraries less.[10]

The third, and still the most popular type with the more conservative novelists, was the ladylike, submissive, slightly pathetic governess. She survives in the novels of Mrs. Henry Wood, of Miss Yonge and in the mild, gentle tales of Miss Anne Thackeray. The heroine of *The Village on the Cliff* (1867) is as touchingly dependent a little governess as ever needed to be propped up between the stiff boards of a three-volume novel. She was 'a blushing eager little thing—attempting to teach children a great many things she had never learned herself'.

Trollope, who had shaken his head kindly over the entire absence of backbone in a Miss Thackeray heroine, came very near to providing another such with his forgiving little governess, Lucy Morris:

Lucy was not beautiful, hardly even pretty—small, in appearance almost insignificant, quite penniless—a governess! He had often asked himself what it was that had so vanquished him. She always wore a pale grey frock with perhaps a grey ribbon—never running to any bright form of clothing. She was educated—very well educated—but she owned no great accomplishment. Yet he had found her out and knew her. He had recognised the treasure and greatly desired to possess it.[11]

Even with all her tears and smiles and gentleness, Lucy is redeemed by the normal, family attributes of a Trollope heroine —common-sense, pluck and determination. When Lady Fawn points out to her how unsuitable it is for a governess to think of marrying a rising young M.P., Lucy has a sufficiently high opinion of herself to refuse to give up her claim to this love.

'It makes me unhappy when I see your mind engaged about Mr. Greystock. There is the truth, Lucy. You should not think of Mr. Greystock. Mr. Greystock is a man who has his way to make in the world and could not marry you even if under other circumstances he would wish to do so . . . Lucy Morris is to us our own dear, dear little friend, Lucy. But Mr. Greystock, who is a Member of Parliament, could not marry a governess.'

'But I love him so dearly', said Lucy, getting up from her chair, 'that his slightest word is to me more than all the words of all the world besides. It is no use, Lady Fawn, I do love him and I don't mean to try to give it up.' . . . Lady Fawn stood silent for a moment and then suggested it would be better for them both to go to bed. During that minute she had been unable to decide what she had better say or do in the present emergency.[12]

Not all novelists were as ready as Trollope to pronounce a benediction upon a match between a governess and an eligible young man. There is considerable disparity of opinion in the novels as to whom a governess may, with propriety, marry. The danger of her forming a *parti* with a younger son is constantly referred to and, while some objected to such a match on financial grounds, others expressed disapproval of her marrying out of her class. The French governess, Geneviève, in *The Young Stepmother*, is considered a quite unsuitable wife for the son of a retired East India civil servant.

'Away from this place she might marry well.'
'Anyone's son but yours,' said Albinia, smiling.
'. . . I was not thinking of anyone in our rank of life. There are many superior men in trade with whom she might be happy.'[13]

Mr. Kendal suggests a superior man in trade; Lady Fawn, a poor clergyman; Lord Cumnor, in *Wives and Daughters*, makes the pompous pronouncement that he can think of no more suitable match for their governess, Clare, than their local medical man.* But, on the other hand, dangerously democratic tendencies are visible from time to time. In a minor novel of 1862, *Abel Drake's Wife*, the heroine Barbara who has risen, by her desire for learning and independence, from factory girl to governess in a rich family is welcomed as a wife for the young son and heir . . . Barbara is noteworthy as one of the few examples in the novel of those underbred young women, referred to by the 1848 *Quarterly Review*, who were creeping into a profession that was not theirs by right of birth and misfortunes.

The earlier propaganda on the governess' behalf had had— and was still having—a considerable effect upon the attitude of

---

* Although Lord Cumnor's viewpoint is ostensibly pre-Victorian, governess and doctor (if unfashionable) were commonly considered to have a social equivalence in the Victorian age.
Cf., Captain Clarence Baker, in *Lovel the Widower* (1860): ' "Attachment between governess and Sawbones?"—"A very fitting match." '

employers to their governesses. Persecution, at least in the novel, had by the sixties given place almost entirely to patronage. The lessons conveyed by twenty-year-old novels, however, still held significance for many. In Lady Amberley's diary of 1868, there is an entry to the effect that she

'read Agnes Grey, one of the Brontës, and should like to give it to every family with a governess and shall read it through again when I have a governess to remind me to be human.'[14]

Both of Collins' governesses—Miss Gwilt of *Armadale* (1866) and Miss Garth of *No Name* (1862)—are in the privileged position of having courtesy shown them as their due. Plans, for instance, for the reception of Miss Gwilt in the family's absence are elaborate:

'If the governess comes to-day let's have her at the picnic. When the governess comes to the cottage, let her find a nice little note of apology (along with the cold fowl or whatever else they give her after her journey), begging her to join us at the picnic and putting a carriage at her own sole disposal to take her there . . . Gad, Sir! She must be a Touchy One if she thinks herself neglected after that!'

Although it would be unwise, in consideration of Collins' habit of exaggerating contemporary trends, to conclude that the offering of cold chicken provides any very reliable drumstick for measuring the extent to which public opinion had shifted its ground since the forties, it is at least an indication that governesses were now being allowed the luxury of feelings, like any other human being. Miss Garth, on the other hand, may be regarded as giving a fairly accurate picture of that ideal relationship between governess and employer which feminists and governesses alike were hoping to establish. She is not the heroine of the novel, but a middle-aged North-country woman.

The self-possession of her progress downstairs and the air of habitual authority with which she looked about her spoke well for her position in Mr. Vanstone's family. This was evidently not one of the forlorn, persecuted, pitiably dependent order of governesses. Here was a woman who lived on ascertained and honourable terms with her employers—a woman who looked capable of sending any parents in England to the right about if they failed to rate her at her proper value.

So far removed was the governess tributary from the main

stream of the women's education movement that practically the same qualifications were required of—and professed by—a governess in the sixties as in the thirties. Miss Clara Mordaunt, an 1839 product without the advantages of a lectures-to-ladies course, would have felt no hesitation in replying to an 1861 advertisement in a novel for a governess, qualified in 'all branches of a solid and polite English education, with music, singing, dancing, callisthenic exercises, theology and the use of the globes'. She might have felt somewhat dubious about theology and the new science of callisthenics which had replaced the earlier rigours of boards upon young ladies' backs and thistles under young ladies' chins—but the familiar ring of 'music, singing, dancing and the use of the globes' would have reassured her.

Any study of the Victorian governess would be incomplete without some reference to those ladies who pursued a middle course, between progressive feminists on the one hand and retrograde dependents on the other—the daily governesses. With, in most cases, no especial liking for their wage-earning existence, but forced to tolerate it by home circumstances, they approximated more nearly to visiting masters than to residential governesses, who seldom had regular hours of duties. A higher standard of education might be looked for among them, as employers naturally demanded value for their money when paying a governess by the hour instead of by the year. The most detailed study of a daily governess is found in a novel that, even in 1861, must have occupied a very subaltern position in the monstrous regiment of minor fiction. *The Daily Governess* or *Self-Dependence*, by Mrs. Gordon Smythies—even taking into account its incredible villain, Sir Jasper, its fantastically beautiful heroine, Lucy Blair, its heightened romance and melodramatic crudities —has much of interest to commend it.

Its value lies in the surprisingly realistic contemporary picture it presents of the life of a daily governess in London. More attention is directed towards the difficulties of the private life of the governess than to her actual duties—to the ignominies and dangers that did not exist for a residential governess, of unescorted walks through London streets, of struggles for a place in crowded omnibuses or third-class railway carriages. It is as she trudges to

work, under a 'large, Gamp-like umbrella', that we are first introduced to the heroine:

We have said that it was no day for ladies; and yet if gentle birth
and breeding, a noble spirit, a pure heart, a pious, cultivated, accomplished mind, self-control, self-dependence, self-possession and perfect
manners constitute a lady then this poor step-child of fortune, this
pretty delicate Lucy Blair, this Daily Governess, battling at once
with Fate and with rough weather on the 25th of March of the Year
of our Lord, 1858, was a lady indeed!

It is interesting to find, at last, in this novel, an acknowledg-
ment of the importance of education in achieving independence
of spirit. It is because Lucy has had a 'brilliant education' at
foreign boarding schools, because she is fully aware of the
marketable value of her knowledge, that she refuses to be beaten
down to housemaid's wages, and commands—for three hours'
tuition per day—the unusually high salary of thirty shillings a
week.* Confident that, with her qualifications, she will have no
difficulty in obtaining another post, she stands up firmly to her
employer when she is threatened with dismissal, in a manner
that would have gladdened the hearts of the founders of Queen's
College.

'I made my début as a daily governess in this house a fortnight ago,
madam; and if, as you anticipate, the young ladies will not be able
to attend to their studies at present I am quite ready to resign the
office. I have many more applications and—forgive me for saying so—
some which promise more docility in the pupils and more sympathy
in the parents.'

The life, even of a well-educated and self-sufficient governess,
however, still had plenty of humiliations and pinpricks. One
passage of arms between Lucy and an insolent child, deals with
a point of etiquette, which must have been only one of many
cruxes that arose and by which the modern reader is continually
finding himself surprised.

Lucy's cheeks were flushed and her spirit rose at these insults but

* The heroine of *The Channings* (Mrs. Henry Wood, 1862)—who
goes out as a daily governess—feels justified in asking only forty guineas
a year because of her youth and inexperience, although she works for
eight hours a day.

she felt it was beneath her to take any notice of them. On the upper landing little Norah O'Blarney came up to her and said:

'Does a daily governess give a single knock or a ring, Miss Blair?'

'A Daily Governess is a lady, my dear', said Lucy kindly, 'and gives a double knock.'

No more adequate summing up of a survey of the Victorian governess could be found than those words of Lucy's—'A governess is a lady'. They explain her reluctance to break the delicate, silver, slightly rusted chains that bound her to her past and forge herself with strong, iron ones to the future. They account for much of her unhappiness but also for her exasperating complacency. They set her irrevocably apart from the feminists who were content to forget their claims as ladies in furthering their rights as women. They are, at once, her epitaph and her extenuation.

CHAPTER III

Woman at Work

1. THE UN-IDEA'D SEX

WITHOUT the governess, the mid-Victorian novel is found to have lost much of the pseudo-educational character her presence imparted to it. Considering how dominant a role the new educational ideas of the '50's and '60's played in feminist history, it might seem at first sight surprising that they had so little effect upon the contemporary novel. For such was indeed the case. Here and there, it is true, we do come upon a novelist who is aware of the revolutionary nature of the movement and in tune with its ideals, but, on the whole, the novel of the period remained unaffected by it.

The reason is not hard to find. There was nothing new about agitation for women's education. The postulate had long since been granted that a certain amount of education—enough at least to enable her to appreciate her husband's acumen—was an excellent thing in woman. There was no clear-cut issue at stake —as in the agitation for suffrage or for a single moral standard— to invest the education movement with appeal as topical novel-material. The subject was vast and confusing. Feminists and anti-feminists were in agreement upon certain points, but while some went all the way in advocating university education for women, others parted company at the cross-roads of secondary education. Even within the pioneer ranks there was dissension, for Miss Davies, abhorring 'female education' was striving to fasten on to women the existing arbitrary standards of masculine learning which the Sidgwicks deplored. The actual mechanics of the movement, too, were bulky and prosaic, and throughout the '50's, while Miss Beale, Miss Buss and Mme. Bodichon were reforming secondary schools,* throughout the '60's, while Miss

* In 1850 the North London Collegiate School (Miss Buss) was founded, followed in 1854 by Cheltenham Ladies' College (Miss Beale, 1858). Other enterprises of the '50's were Mme. Bodichon's co-educa-

Davies was besieging Cambridge, the topic of higher education
for women recurred more frequently in letters, articles and
speeches than in three-volume novels from Mudie's. In progressive circles, it was a conversational standby. By 1872, Lady
Amberley was writing complacently to her daughter: 'I have not
had time to read the article in *The Times* on female education
. . . I hear young men are much afraid women shall know too
much and spoil the race by overworking their brains—poor dears,
they will ever find fools to match them.'[1]

On the one hand, there were too few concrete achieve-
ments to interest the novelist—it was not until 1873 that Miss
Davies shepherded her girls through Cambridge streets to take
their unofficial part in the Tripos examinations; on the other, the
ideals of the movement were too elevated for anyone less philosophical than George Eliot to attempt to expound. The aim of
higher education for women, according to Miss Davies' manifesto of 1866, was to 'produce women of the best and highest
type', to encourage a disinterested love of knowledge and to
prove that there lay between the sexes 'a deep and broad basis
of likeness'.[2] These aspirations could scarcely be expected to
awake an immediate, sympathetic response in the heart of the
popular novelist. Only a woman could know the chafing disquiet
felt by other intelligent women at the narrow bounds of female
knowledge and do justice to the mental conflicts of those oppressed by their own ignorance. And as for the broad basis of
likeness between the sexes—the coping stone of the novel for
over a century had been the essential dissimilarity of the hero
and heroine.

There had, it is true, been a notable exception in the novels of
Jane Austen, in which all the characters moved easily about on
the same plane and, men and women alike, were judged entirely
on their merits and foibles. There could, for instance, be no point
of precedence between Lady Bertram's torpor and Robert Ferrar's
'strong, natural, sterling insignificance', no doubt about the ab-
surdity of giving Mr. Collins unlimited power in marriage over
Elizabeth Bennet—or even over Charlotte—because of the for-

tional school and Octavia Hill's combined work-room and school for
poorer girls. The Girls' Public Day Schools Trust did not operate until
1872.

tuitous circumstance of his sex. Mary Wollstonecraft's passionate disbelief in 'sexual vices and virtues'—one of the main shots in the anti-feminist artillery—was dispassionately borne out in Jane Austen's novels. After encountering Anne's loyalty and fortitude, Mr. Woodhouse's timidity, Sir Walter Elliot's feline vanity, Emma's candour, Mrs. Palmer's prattling foolishness and John Thorpe's foolish rattling, it must have been difficult to avoid drawing the implication that the resemblance between the sexes was greater than their disparity, that to a large extent their vices and virtues were interchangeable.

But still, many years later, feminists were making little headway in persuading the public of the truth of this point, made so effortlessly by Miss Austen. Consequently, it is only in the writings of a few women novelists of the time that we find any attempt at apprehending and putting on record the frustrated feminine cravings which were to be discerned at the core of the educational movement, which were so out of place in the social novel and were so eagerly seized upon, later in the century, when the psychological novel was coming into its own.

Miss Davies' insistence upon the points of resemblance between men and women is explained by looking back some twenty years to 1847, when higher education for women got off to a bad start with the publication of *The Princess*, a poem which the anti-feminists appropriated to flutter at their mast for a long time to come. Ironically enough, Tennyson had intended the poem to advance the cause of women's education and, indeed, had his treatment of the university theme been serious and sympathetic no better propaganda for organised education could have been devised. A residential college with violet-hooded doctors, gowned students, complicated courses in every subject (anatomy excepted) and a sorority motto, 'Power through Knowledge', was a project far more ambitious than Miss Davies dared to dream of. But Tennyson, firmly convinced that 'if women ever were to play such freaks the burlesque and the tragic might go hand-in-hand',[3] merely raised his elaborate mediæval structure so high the better to enjoy the crash when the moment came for him to expose its faulty foundations and to send the edifice toppling to the ground. As a result, the Victorian reading public felt at full liberty to enjoy the beauties of the poem, the gentle ridicule, 'Prudes for proctors, dowagers for deans', the patronising appro-bation, the generous admiration—secure in the certainty of an ultimate *éclaircissement*. Nor were they disappointed when it came. The couplet with which Tennyson summed up his doc-trines was admirably suited to Victorian taste and helped to place masculine education for women in an unfavourable light for many years. It had all been said before, to be sure, but never so well, never so succinctly.

> For woman is not undevelop't man,
> But diverse . . .

Victoria herself was graciously pleased to approve Mr. Tenny-son's sentiments. Where the Queen led, her subjects were not far behind, and so the gospel of *The Princess** was absorbed into the nation's consciousness—a gospel with much in it that was pro-gressive and tolerant but one admirably calculated to discourage any real attempt at levelling-up women's education with that of men. As long as the basis of likeness between men and women was denied there could be no common educational standard. So that Miss Davies, coming fresh to the educational battleground some two decades later, felt—and rightly—that until the tenets which *The Princess* had underlined in Victorian minds were rooted out, Little-Go and Tripos examinations were far outside her grasp.

It was especially the manly subjects, the classics and sciences, to which the educationists longingly turned their eyes, and, although the vast majority of novel-heroines were still to be found pursuing their accomplishments and more elegant studies, there stands out, here and there, such a young lady as Argemone Lavington.

What was Argemone doing all this time? Argemone was busy in her boudoir . . . among books and statuettes, and dried flowers, fancying herself, and not unfairly, very intellectual. She had four new manias every year; her last winter's one had been that bottle-and-squirt mania, miscalled chemistry; her spring madness was for the Greek drama; she had devoured Schlegel's lectures, and thought them

* By 1850 the poem was so well-known that Kingsley considered it unnecessary to quote from a work so familiar to all his readers.

divine; and now she was hard at work on Sophocles, with a little help
from translations, and thought she understood him every word.[4]

On the face of it, one might think, a lighthearted dilettante
approach. But Kingsley's Argemone is a *Princess* in prose—
conceived, he protested, many years before Tennyson's heroine
—a young lady who 'had worshipped intellect and now it
had become her tyrant'. Like the Princess, she is taught her
lesson:

She was matched, for the first time, with a man who was her own
equal in intellect and knowledge: and she felt how real was that
sexual indifference which she had been accustomed to consider as
an insolent calumny against woman. Proudly and indignantly she
struggled against the conviction, but in vain . . . Her mind was beside his as the vase of cut flowers by the side of the rugged tree, whose
roots are feeding deep into the mother earth. [But] on all points
which touched the heart he looked up to her as infallible and inspired
. . . and thus, half unconsciously to himself, he taught her where her
true kingdom lay—that the heart, and not the brain, enshrines the
priceless pearl of womanhood.[5]

On the whole, Charlotte Brontë was inclined to agree with
Kingsley on this point. Once their hearts are given to the men
of their choice, her heroines are always ardently disposed to
acknowledge them their masters. There could be no doubt as to
the calibre of mind that Shirley was taking into marriage—
Shirley, the shrewd and intelligent, transacting business, going
over her accounts, talking politics and religion, priding herself
on her manly qualities—'I read the leading articles, and the
foreign intelligence, and I look over the market prices; in
short, I read just what gentlemen read.' But once Shirley has
met her match she is proud to resign from her rank of Captain Keeldar, master of her own fate, and to assume a subaltern
role.

None the less, the intellectual pretensions of even the most
womanly women grew with the passing years. Miss Yonge, who
deplored the idea of university education for women and was
anti-feminist to the backbone, did not scruple to give her best-
known heroine, Ethel May, a conspicuously masculine understanding of Greek and Latin and a keener aptitude for advanced

studies than her brother. Elizabeth Barrett Browning, in her verse-novel of 1857, wrapped her Aurora Leigh in a

> . . . large
> Man's doublet, careless did it fit or no.

and calling down scorn upon the liberal education of woman-hood—the classical French, the German, the polka, the stuffed birds, the waxed flowers—let her acquire 'the trick of Latin and Greek'. But no more than the trick. It was upon poetry that Aurora satisfied her appetite after ardently nibbling her way through the classics. When she found the poets, her 'soul sprang up surprised'. The preliminary training with the classics may, of course, have imparted elasticity to her soul, but the stress throughout the poem is laid rather on Aurora's insight into life, as an artist, than upon her intellectual expansion, and it is to the heroines of George Eliot that we must turn to find young women looking to knowledge above all for strength and exhibit-ing a most touching faith in the power of Latin and Greek to solve the riddle of the universe for them.

It was not entirely out of devotion to her future husband that Dorothea wished to know Latin and Greek. Those provinces of masculine knowledge seemed to her a standing ground from which all truth could be seen more truly. As it was, she constantly doubted her own conclusions, because she felt her own ignorance; how could she be confident that one-roomed cottages were not for the glory of God, when men who knew the classics appeared to conciliate indiffer-ence to the cottages with zeal for the glory? Perhaps even Hebrew might be needed—at least the alphabet and a few roots—in order to arrive at the core of things and judge soundly on the social duties of the Christian.[6]

Maggie Tulliver, as well as Dorothea Brooke, was eager to strike out into deeper waters than the shallows of ladies' school literature.

Even at school she had often wished for books with more in them; everything she learned there seemed like the ends of long threads that snapped immediately . . . No dream world would satisfy her now; . . . she wanted some key that would enable her to understand and in understanding, endure, the heavy weight that had fallen on her young heart. If she had been taught 'real learning and wisdom,

such as great men knew', she thought she should have held the secrets
of life; if she had only books, that she might learn for herself what
wise men knew! . . . Still Latin, Euclid and Logic would surely be a
considerable step in masculine wisdom—in that knowledge which
made men contented and even glad to live . . . And so the poor
child . . . filling her vacant hours with Latin, geometry and the
forms of the syllogism, and feeling a gleam of triumph every now
and then that her understanding was quite equal to these peculiarly
masculine studies . . . was as lonely in her trouble as if she had been
the only girl in the civilised world of that day who had come out of
her school life with a soul untrained for inevitable struggles—with
no other part of her inherited share in the hard-won treasures of
thought . . . than shreds and patches of feeble literature and false
history . . . but unhappily quite without that knowledge of the
irreversible laws within and without her, which, governing the habits,
becomes morality, and, developing the feelings of submission and
dependence, becomes religion.[7]

Just as Aurora 'found the poets', so Maggie came upon the
little volume of St. Thomas à Kempis, which did more to satisfy
her hungry heart than all the logarithms and syllogisms she had
been tackling—but both from Mrs. Browning and George Eliot
can be gained some idea of the unhappy state of mind of
thoughtful young women of that time who, casting around for
something to explain their restless cravings, believed that in the
closed volume of education was to be found the secret of their
discontent.

These authoresses, diametrically opposed on many points, were
in agreement in their attitude towards other, less exceptional
women—'By their works shall ye know them.' Carvers of their
own destiny, they saw no reason why other women should not
prove their mettle in action rather than talk. Similarly, their
equally remarkable heroines set about achieving their intellectual
emancipation with a resolute independence of purpose which
can scarcely be considered representative of the normal feminine
outlook on education. More normal women were, of course, considerably less vocal on educational matters and pursuit, through
the mid-Victorian scene, of the chimæra of an average novelist
with an average heroine, who yet had carefully formulated views
on education, might well have proved disappointing. But to the
Victorian novel all things are possible, and when, in 1871, Mrs.

Jane Brookfield wrote her novel, *Influence*, she provided a
heroine who not only fulfils these requirements—but fulfils them
at unstinted length.

Mrs. Brookfield, though a remarkable woman in many ways,
was no literary genius. Of her novels, mainly the products of her
widowhood, it can be said that they are no worse than those of
countless other women of the time whose 'application of feminine
incapacity to literature' George Eliot found 'more piteous almost
than soapless poverty'.[8] She shone most brightly in her domestic
circle. It was her warmth and wit, her beauty and kindness, and
not the puissance of her pen that attracted to her house (free
from both the gusty draughts of feminism and the stuffiness of
feme-coverte domesticity) such men of letters as Tennyson, Carlyle and Thackeray.[9] Partly responsible for the conception of
Amelia Sedley, she yet deplored Amelia's lack of brains;* and
as the admiring wife of a fashionable preacher, she yet made him
appear superficial in comparison. So that it is not surprising that,
although she herself was happy in marriage, she was fully aware
of the problems that were facing young women like her heroine,
Alice.

It is the old argument that much learning is detrimental to
her chances of marriage that Alice has to counter in her family
circle. Like Celia Brooke, who regarded learning as 'a kind of
damp which might in due time saturate a neighbouring body',
they looked on erudition with suspicion.

When Alice tried to please Mary by reading downstairs, the books
she was interested in came under Mary's most serious condemnation
as fit only for men. J. S. Mill's works for instance were, she knew,
a most radical set of books—indeed, Sir Edward had said of all
Mill's writings that they deserved to be burned by the common
hangman.

'And I suppose you will admit, my dear Alice,' Lady Peachey said,
'that Edward must know better than any woman can do what is fit
for us to read or not. Edward says that all women need go in for is to
be *au courant* with the literature of the day.'

* 'The last number of *Vanity Fair* is exceedingly good, I think, but
I begin to wish he would give Amelia a few more brains . . . and
though he has the right amount of anti-phlegm and affectionateness he
really is an uncommonly dull and selfish character.'

'I do not set up to be a blue-stocking,' Alice said. 'I read for my own benefit and not to please other people.'

'But not Lewes on Philosophy or Herbert Spencer's Essays . . . they won't help you a bit in practical life.'

By her lover, too, who shows an unworthy tendency to equate strength of mind, an aquiline nose and college education, Alice is humoured rather than encouraged in her scheme for systematised knowledge.

'Indeed, I dislike and shrink from the idea of acquiring influence—but I should like to understand where I am going and upon what principle I am to be directed. If I were better educated I should be able to judge whether women are ill-used or not. As it is I know I have no right to express any opinion about it . . . in fact, at this moment I should like to be given a college education more than anything in the world . . .'

'Well, if you care to acquire it you have opportunities and facilities enough opened to you now on all sides. There are lectures on purpose for Ladies both at Cambridge and London, why don't you attend them?' Frank said kindly.

'I do, of course, I do,' Alice answered, 'but I don't get enough out of them to satisfy all that I want. They remind me of old-fashioned books adapted for children; like *Selections from the Schoolroom*. You see, the lectures we have are not arranged systematically enough to become a regular education for us. For instance, we may have a course of lectures on mathematics perhaps, and just as we are beginning to delight in the subject and to be absorbed in it the course ends and may not be taken up again for months. This is not serious education, is it? It is exactly like reading extracts from different authors and never getting through the books themselves . . . Mama wishes very much that girls could join in the lectures at the college (University College) and really be educated there, but there seems to be a difficulty about it . . . I believe ladies may go to any of the short courses of lectures in the evening there, but they may not go through the whole system of education nor attend at the classes in the day time with the other students.'

Bearing in mind that Mamma, who wishes her daughter to have a university education, is a fragile, clinging woman, and that Alice herself is in love and heading towards marriage when she utters her gallant words, it will be seen that the process of

5

edging love and marriage from the commanding positions they had held so long was just beginning to get under way. Alice, it is true, was quite content to give up her college project in favour of marriage with Frank, but these were early days, and, at least, she had expressed herself freely and shown herself to have other thoughts in her head than matrimony. The un-idea'd sex, in fact, was gradually realising its urgent need of abstract ideas. George Eliot, in 1870, had summed up the position in a letter to Mrs. Lytton:

'We women are always in danger of living too exclusively in the affections; and though our affections are perhaps the best gifts we have, we ought also to have our share of the more independent life—some joy in things for their own sake. It is piteous to see the helplessness of some sweet women when their affections are disappointed—because all their teaching has been, that they can only delight in study of any kind for the sake of a personal love. They have never contemplated an independent delight in ideas as an experience which they could confess without being laughed at. Yet surely women need this sort of defence against passionate affliction even more than men.'

In the years that followed, women became more and more conscious of this need, and it was not only women novelists that found interest in the unsatisfied desires of their sex. During this early period, however, it was revolutionary action rather than revolutionary thought that appealed to the novel-reading public, so that, if an advanced woman were to enter into the novelist's scheme of things at all, she was far more likely to do so in the role of Career Woman—a role that had a definite label attached to it. In this matter of careers for women there could be—and were—two decided groups of opinion. It was, therefore, on this controversial issue with its clear, easily-grasped outlines, that the novelist seized while paying scant attention to the march of the education movement, from one milestone to another through the sixties, straight up to the gates of Girton . . .

2. FEMALE WORKMEN

The year 1857 is of significance, for it was then that the Association for the Promotion of the Employment of Women set up its Bureau in Langham Place in connection with the

Englishwomen's Journal. In other words, women workers who, till then, had been enduring wretched conditions for miserable wages—supported in their travail by the ponderous sympathy of the Victorian middle classes—were from that time given feminist backing. Although this eventually meant that more jobs were opened to them and that agitation for higher wages was set afoot, a more immediate result was the withdrawal of the pity which the British public had comfortably offered for so long. The exchange was not for the worse, although many helpless women, who were quite as reluctant to turn out into the streets and earn their living after 1857 as ever they had been before, may well have felt bewildered to hear themselves roundly condemned as feminists. It was, however, the presence in the wage-earning ranks of a growing body of women, eager to be independent and support themselves, that gave colour to the idea that every working woman brought female emancipation a step nearer, that every additional shop-assistant or clerk was a triumph for the cause. Nor was this far from the truth. It was at this crux in the performance of the Victorian career woman that episodic, pathetic scenes suddenly switched over to strong feminist drama—to the pained surprise of the audience and not a few of the actresses.

The employment position at the beginning of the Victorian age is fairly comprehensively indicated in an article by Lady Ellis, 'The Education of Young Ladies for Other Occupations than Teaching' (1838). At the time of writing the only work considered suitable for a lady was that of teaching, although many 'females of gentility' supported themselves in ways frowned upon by society—in engraving, watch-making, painting, carving, gilding—strictly in the privacy of their own drawing-rooms. Lady Ellis boldly advocated the entry of women into skilled trades.

Any suggestion on the propriety of teaching trades is treading upon delicate ground. Prejudices and habits of the age are opposed to such a practice, but the great question is—is it right? Would it tend to good? Would it add to the happiness of the female portion of society? And if so, it is our duty to endeavour to overcome the prejudices.[10]

Twenty years later Lady Ellis would have had more chance of an attentive hearing but, in the meantime, as Harriet Martineau pointed out in *Deerbrook*, the 'tutor, the tailor and the hatter' continued to be the only occupations that the gently-bred with propriety might pursue and only the first was secure from the intrusion of the lower classes. Before 1857 the national conscience was no less than four times, in fairly rapid succession, pricked out of its complacent torpor by revelations about women wage-earners. First, by milliners, then by factory women, next by governesses and finally by nurses. The agitations on behalf of milliners and factory girls were practically contemporary. The tailors' strike was followed by the efforts of the Christian Socialists on behalf of tailoresses; and in 1844 the Association for the aid and benefit of Dressmakers and Milliners was formed. But, as the co-operative workrooms in which Maurice put his faith were a failure, the milliners, having had their moment in the limelight, were forced to wait for succour till alternative employments were opened to them. In much the same way, the miserable women who, after the disclosures of Shaftesbury's pit and factory Commissions of 1842 and 1847, were thrown into even more degrading conditions of unemployment, had a shroud of neglect wrapped round them until the Government enquiry forty years later. It was while the agitation was at its height, and Victorian hearts were at their most susceptible, that several novels appeared to champion the cause of the working-girl and, for a time, the milliner and the factory-hand had unrivalled best-selling appeal. But by the early fifties the spotlight, as we have seen, was moving round to the governess; Miss Nightingale's Crimean nurses were the heroines of the moment; and the novel of the work-room and factory lost its popularity.

So far, then, it had been the hardships and injustices of the position of women wage-earners that had occupied the public's mind. Women who were not forced to work but preferred a profession to dependence on others were new, alarming phenomena that deserved no sympathy. Had it been more generally realised that Miss Nightingale was not so much a beautiful legend as a ruthless administrator and reformer, that she used the Crimean War as a means of satisfying the desire she had had since she was six years old—'for something to fill and employ all my faculties—a profession, a trade, a necessary occupation', her reputation might have sheltered the feminists from much of the storm of ridicule and protest that broke upon them when they opened their Employment Bureau. But, as it was, the nation persisted in regarding her as an embodiment of the angelic self-sacrifice that the wives and mothers of England modestly claimed as their own outstanding characteristic and even when, in 1857, she founded the Nightingale School of Nurses and forced her crisply-starched ideas of hygiene and discipline down their throats, it was only the weaker* stomachs that suffered any digestive upset.

Nursing, then, was a profession apart and needed no other advocate than Miss Nightingale. The Employment Bureau had plenty to do in opening up other professions without encroaching on her sphere, for the 1851 census had revealed alarming numbers of single, self-dependent women. It was their aim to help women to find any work whatever that they could successfully cope with—as clerks, shop-assistants, telegraphists, compositors—to better the conditions of domestic servants, needle-women and factory hands, to encourage the adventurous to taste the joys of independence. It was their last aim that linked the employment and education movements together and incurred especial disapproval from onlookers. It was one thing to help women of the employee class to find work; quite another to enlist women from the higher social classes to the professional ranks. By 1861, considerable progress had been made in the number of jobs open to women, according to an article published in that year—'What are Women Doing.'[11] The money-earning classes were divided into three sections by the writer. In the first and largest, with wages presumably at subsistence level, she slumped together in a democratic sisterhood, actresses, singers, hair-dressers, telegraphists and teachers; the next section consisted merely of domestic servants and the third of factory-girls and milliners. But at least the choice of employment was growing

* A literary notice of *Notes on Nursing* (F. Nightingale), in the *Ladies' Treasury* of 1860, reveals a certain squeamishness Miss Nightingale herself would have scorned: 'The second circumstance of surprise and regret to us in the perusal of these otherwise excellent notes is a certain spirit of harshness and contempt, evident in the phraseology of the book—at times even becoming, not only ungracious, but (we write it with regret) wanting in *Good Taste.*'

wider. The arts were now being more depended on as a resource
for bread; in 1858 the assault on the medical profession had
begun and Miss Davies and others were soon trying hard to co-
relate in the minds of the stoutly-resisting Victorian public the
ideas of education and employment for women. For Miss Davies
was quite clear in her own mind that her 'highest and best type
of woman' was admirably fitted by her education for work in
hospitals and reformatories, penitentiaries and nurseries, school-
rooms, factories and farms in an administrative capacity or for
the medical and literary professions. If the abstract aims of the
educationists had seemed harmless enough, the concrete uses to
which they suggested higher education should be put were quite
a different matter and voices were upraised in outraged disapproval when once the implications of careers for middle-class
women had been fully grasped. *The What-not* or *Ladies' Handy
Book* for 1859-60, for instance, exercised heavy sarcasm on the
topic:

'Oh, my dear aunt,' exclaimed a young and lively looking lady, 'I
have just come from hearing a lecture on *female workmen* by Miss
B., whose surgical and anatomical lectures I attended with so much
pleasure last season; so striking; so convincing. She showed that
nothing more is necessary but that every young girl should be taught
a trade and thus rendered independent of the brutal male sex and we
shall hear no more of female crime and wretchedness; no more need
of reformatories and penitentiaries . . .'

Much more in the same vein was to follow, but it would have
taken more than *The What-Not's* ridicule to divert the career
woman from her course. None the less, as can be seen from even
this brief extract, she lent herself admirably to satire and jour-
nalists and novelists did not fail to take advantage of this gra-
tuitous accession to their facetious stock: she provided far more
stimulating material than her less spirited predecessor, the lower-
class working woman, with whom the novelist, before 1857, had
had to be content.

For, in spite of the number of novels that the hardships of
factory girls and milliners inspired, it cannot be said that any of
them approached the subject from a noticeably feminist as well
as humanitarian angle. Mary Barton, for instance, entertained no

lofty ideas about the dignity of female labour. She was glad to be a milliner because it would have been worse to have been a factory girl and she was at least called 'young lady' by the slave-driver to whom she was apprenticed. But, although she would much have preferred to be married than earning her living so painfully, she had enough of the proper pride of the working woman to spurn Mr. Carson's honourable intentions.

'I am obliged to you, Sir, for telling me what you have. You may think I am a fool: but I did think you meant to marry me all along, and yet, thinking so I felt I could not love you . . . Now, sir, I tell you, if I had loved you before I don't think I should have loved you now you have told me you meant to ruin me; for that's the plain English of not meaning to marry me till just this minute.'[12]

In such words—liable to make Pamela turn distractedly in her grave—is heard the new note of independence that is audible also in the remarks of Disraeli's working-women in *Sybil* (1845)—in which we are given a realistic glimpse of young girls enjoying their earnings, preferring to keep house on their own rather than support their parents, savouring their new-found importance, even while taking an intelligent interest in their wrongs.

'We'll have the rights of labour yet; the ten-hour bill, no fines and no individuals admitted to any work who have not yet completed their sixteenth year.'
'No, fifteen,' said Caroline eagerly . . .

As long as the work is imperative, the novelist is, in every case, on the side of the working woman, but, as soon as there is a suspicion of her getting any satisfaction out of her self-supporting existence, the forces of anti-feminism are rallied. Disraeli makes his attitude quite clear in respect of married women working away from home.

We have removed woman from her sphere; we may have reduced wages by her introduction into the market of labour; but under these circumstances what we call domestic life is a condition impossible to be realised for the people of this country.

And from the Ladies' Gallery, in somewhat less elevated language, Mrs. Gaskell supported Disraeli's point.

'Father does not like women to work in factories,' said Mary.

'No, I know he does not and reason good. They oughtn't to go after they're married that I'm very clear about. I could reckon up—ay, nine men I know as has been driven to the public house by having wives as worked in factories . . . I wish our Jem could say a word to the Queen about factory work for married women. Eh! but he comes it strong when once you get him to speak about it. Wife of his'n will never work away fra' home.'

The brief sojourn of the novel heroine in the factory and workroom or at the pit-head was patently considered by novelists to be quite extrinsic to any development in their ideal of woman-hood. And even less were they affected by the wave of enthusiasm for the nursing profession that swept England in the early fifties. Mrs. Gamp was not entirely banished, as might have been ex-pected, from the novel after the foundation of the Nightingale School of Nurses. When her prototype appeared, as she did from time to time, she was, however, referred to as 'an inferior class of nurse' to show that the novelist knew of the existence of a better type. In *The Gilberts and their Guests* (1856), the nurse with 'fierce cunning eyes, a harsh voice and repulsive sallow countenance' attempts robbery and murder; in *Hard Cash* (1863), Nurse Hannah is described as 'a muscular young virgin' and 'Baby-face Biceps''; and in *The New Magdalen* (1873) Mercy Merrick differs from her distinguished predecessor, when she offers her services as a nurse in the Franco-Prussian War, in her motive for doing so—as an escape from a life of prostitu-tion.

It cannot be said that the novelists showed excessive reverence for the calling of a sick-nurse in the twenty years following the publication of *Ruth*—a novel often taken as an illustration of the disrepute of nurses in the pre-Nightingale era. 'A person unfit for anything else may move quietly and speak gently and give medicine when the doctor orders it and keep awake at night; and those are the best qualities I ever heard of in a sick nurse,'[13] said Jemima to Ruth—and it was only very gradually that any-thing more ambitious was demanded of her. Miss Nightingale was too much of a heroine *in propria persona* to induce novelists to produce weak imitations of her, although there are frequent references to her work in their pages—allusions, indeed, not always complimentary, for she held the nation tantalisingly at arms' length. Rosina Bulwer Lytton, dipping her pen in scented vitriol, as usual, writes in *Very Successful*:

This letter was filled with the most enthusiastic encomiums on the tender care and the sleepless devotion of the lady-nurses at Scutari to all the other sufferers. And yet to read the English newspapers one would think that no other lady besides Miss Nightingale had, like Lord Bateman, put herself all aboard of a ship this foreign country for to see, and that she alone had insisted on dressing all the wounds in all the wards, instead of which never were the beneficial effects of the division of labour more triumphantly exemplified than in the manifold division of this labour of love. Now, why is it that none of her brave corps of volunteers should ever be mentioned?

A less warped outlook than that of Rosina, and one in all probability far more representative of the attitude of most Victorian women to the nursing profession, is that of Trollope's Lady Staveley. When she has rejected Felix Graham as a suitable husband for her daughter, she apprehensively watches Madeline growing more and more pensive and earnest-minded and finds her reading

. . . a paper about sick people, written by Florence Nightingale . . . But it was by no means Lady Staveley's desire that her daughter should take to the Florence Nightingale line of life. The charities of Noningsby were done on a large scale, in a quiet, handsome, method- ical manner and were regarded by the mistress of the mansion as a very material part of her life's duty; but she would have been driven distracted had she been told that a daughter of hers was about to devote herself exclusively to charity . . . Such as she was, whether good or bad, she had no desire whatever that her daughter should withdraw herself from the world and give up to sick women what was meant for mankind . . . Would not Felix Graham be better than no son-in-law? When someone had once very strongly praised Florence Nightingale in Lady Staveley's presence, she had stoutly declared her opinion that it was a young woman's duty to get married. For myself, I am inclined to agree with her.[14]

So far, then, as nurses, milliners and factory girls were con- cerned, mid-Victorian novelists merely brushed the skirts of the issue of women's employment. It was when the more ambitious professions came under consideration—those that might possibly provide an alluring alternative to marriage—that they settled down to the problem with some show of enthusiasm. Acting, painting, writing, journalism, medicine—each was a worthy opponent to marriage—worthy, too, of fluttering the pages of the novel.

3. THE CLEVER WOMAN OF THE FAMILY

Although there are few career-woman novels before 1857, the life-long profession of ministering to man's comfort—the established creed—was attacked vehemently as early as 1848 by one who herself had spent a large portion of her life in following that profession and enjoyed it heartily. Geraldine Jewsbury, that 'scraggly little creature—flimsy tatter', as Carlyle called her, was none the less an impassioned champion of woman's right to develop her own gifts unhindered. In *The Half-Sisters* she espoused the cause of the actress.

Her heroine, Bianca, illegitimate and poor, is helped to fame as an actress by a rich young man, Conrad Percy. After Conrad nas spent some time abroad he finds that his ideal of woman has changed from the gallant, passionate Bianca to her gentle, lady-like half-sister Alice. His friend, Lord Melton, on the other hand, appreciates Bianca's worth and honours her profession— although he finally persuades her to give it up to marry him. As might be expected, much of the book is given over to discussions on the suitability of a profession for a woman:

'A woman', said Conrad, 'who makes her mind public or exhibits herself in any way, no matter how it may be dignified by the title of art, seems to me little better than a woman of a nameless class. I am more jealous of the mind than of the body; and to me there is something revolting in the notion of a woman who professes to love and belong to you alone, going and printing the secrets of her inmost heart, the most sacred workings of her soul, for the benefit of all who can pay for them . . . No wife or daughter of mine should ever, with my consent, form an acquaintance with actress, artist, singer or musician . . . A public life must deteriorate women: they are thrown on the naked world to have to deal like us men, with its hard realities; they lose all the beautiful ideal of their nature, all that is gentle, helpless and confiding . . . A woman's work cannot be judged on the basis of its real merit like that of men; consequently it never is; there is a gallant fiction which guides the judgement. The intrinsic value of a woman's work out of her own sphere is nothing . . . Quietly at

anchor by her own fireside, gentle, low-voiced, loving, confiding—
such is *my* ideal of a woman and a wife and certainly a professional
woman would not be likely to realise it.'

'Bravo,' cried Melton . . . 'I must take a glass of wine to recover
from such a vision of exquisite helplessness . . . Until women cease
to be educated with a sole view to what men admire they will never
be any better than they are. We require virtue and strength and
truth and reality from women; grace and agreeableness are secondary
qualities. I can tolerate a woman with real genius and qualifications
for it following a profession because, to a degree, it gives her a personal and independent existence. Your ideal of a woman would not
stand the wear and tear of life.'

It is Melton who rebukes Bianca for wishing to give up acting
when she finds that she has lost Conrad's love, by telling her that
her gifts were not bestowed on her to make her desirable in the
eyes of any one person. Here Miss Jewsbury is sounding the note
heard again twenty-two years later in George Eliot's letter: 'It
is piteous to see the helplessness of some sweet women when their
affections are disappointed—because all their teaching has been,
that they can only delight in study of any kind for the sake of
a personal love'—and Bianca is emboldened by it to more than
hold her own in subsequent conversation with Melton's less advanced sister:

'Women in general have no settled occupation,' said Bianca, looking up. 'Those who have families have indeed a legitimate occupation, enough to employ all their energies. Those women, too, who have
to gain their own living have their hands pretty full . . . But look at
the great body of unmarried women in the middle-classes. They want
an object, they want a strong purpose and they want an adequate
employment in exchange for precious life . . . I have had too much
struggling—but I have had work to do and I have done it.'

'But, my dear Bianca,' said Lady Vernon, 'you are, like Melton,
keeping to safe generalities. How in the present state of society are
women to be employed? Women's employments are so limited . . .'

'I told you,' said Bianca, 'that there was no compendious receipt to
improve the condition of women; their present position has been of
gradual growth and has all the disadvantages of a transition state—
from bondwomen to ornamental appendages.'

Miss Jewsbury was writing in the late '40's when, indeed, employments for women were considerably more limited. 'Being

on the stage' could, of course, mean many things, and there is
no sign in Dickens or Thackeray that the footlights career of
ballet dancer or chorus girl was held in much esteem. Little
Dorrit's sister, Fanny, is spurned as a match for Mr. Sparkler,
and Elizabeth, the governess in *Lovel the Widower*, who has had
a past in 'blue and spangles', is cast out of the house with con-
tumely by the two grandmothers. As for the Fotheringay, 'legitimate' actress though she is, her proposed union with Pen fills his
uncle with horror. 'We're not going to have a Pendennis, the
head of the house, marry a strolling mountebank from a booth.
No, no, we won't marry into Greenwich Fair, ma'am!'

None of these was the serious artist that Bianca claimed to
be, however, and when, in 1869, William Black put forward
another actress heroine, he claimed that the status of the actress
had risen considerably among thinking people:

'You believe that your mother, a carefully pious and correct lady
who has lived all her life in the country, would dare to admit that she
knew an actress?'
'She would be proud to avow it,' said Will. 'Perhaps the parish
clerk's wife and the vet.'s wife might be shocked, but the educated
and intelligent of them would only be envious of my mother.'[15]

It was not only an actress with whom Conrad Percy had determined to prevent his women-folk associating; a woman-painter
or writer he considered to be equally unsexed. In 1850, Mrs.
Craik, who, though not a feminist in her views, had created some
interest by setting up in London a bachelor-girl establishment
with another young woman, wrote *Olive*—of which Catherine
Winkworth announced with generous determination: 'I mean
to like *Olive* for its author's sake.' The heroine of Mrs. Craik's
novel is a cripple and an artist—not a dabbler, not a perpetrator
of 'young-lady sketches of tumbledown cottages'—but a real self-
supporting painter. 'Though this confession may somewhat
lessen the romance of her character, it was from no yearning
after fame, no genius-led ambition, but from the mere desire of
earning money that Olive Rothesay first conceived the thought
of becoming an artist.'

Because of her infirmity, Olive considers that marriage is
denied to her and so is able to apply herself to her art with no

erotic disturbances to keep her from attaining fame and independence. She feels sufficient pride in her way of life to defend it, in
conversation with a young lady of fashion, from patronage:

'My dear Miss Rothesay,' said Chrystal loftily, 'there is a difference
between a mere artist working for a livelihood and an independent
lady.'
Olive's slight figure expressed unwonted dignity. In her arose something of the old Rothesay pride, but still more of pride in her Art.
'There is a difference, but to my way of thinking it is often on the
side of the artist . . .'

But Olive, like Bianca, does not carry her pride in her art
to the fanatical extreme of refusing marriage from the man she
loves. Both Mrs. Craik and Miss Jewsbury, having shot all their
bolts in the course of the novel, are content in the end to let
their heroines—whose ultimate greatness their readers have not
for one moment been allowed to doubt—sink gently into matrimony. Of Olive, Mrs. Craik comments imperturbably that her
husband's influence is to deprive the Scottish Academy of 'no
one knew how many grand pictures'—while Bianca, after passionately scaling the heights of her profession, is last seen
crocheting a cushion for her sister-in-law. The majority of
feminists would, however, have been quite willing to agree that
marriage was a far better thing on the whole than a career. All
that most of them desired was to have work thrown open to
women who wished to take advantage of it, 'to assist the female
population over a time of difficulty and not to develop a new state
of social life', as the *Englishwomen's Journal* put it. And, in consequence, the brave words of Bianca and Olive would not, taken
in conjunction with their orthodox happy endings, necessarily
have struck even the more advanced of Victorian readers as
incongruous.
It is the emptiness of the lives of most single women that concerns Caroline Helstone and Shirley Keeldar:

'Shirley, men and women are so different; they are in such a different position. Women have so few things to think about—men so
many . . . Much of what cheers your life may be dependent on him,
while not a feeling or interest of moment in his eyes may have reference to you . . .'

'Caroline,' demanded Miss Keeldar abruptly, 'don't you wish you had a profession, a trade?'

'I wish it fifty times a day. As it is, I often wonder what I came into the world for. I long to have something absorbing and compulsory to fill my head and hands and to occupy my thoughts.'

'Can labour alone make a human being happy?'

'No, but it can give varieties of pain, and prevent us from breaking our hearts with a single tyrant master torture. Besides, successful labour has its recompense; a vacant, weary, lonely, hopeless life has none.'[16]

And certainly it is an indication rather of empty days than of any stifled genius that so many Victorian women have a novel to their credit. Miss Yonge, Mrs. Lynn Linton and Mrs. Browning, however—three women who supported themselves by the pen—produced at least one novel each in which the heroine is a 'writing-woman' proper. *Aurora Leigh*, a novel in verse form, gives a detailed impression of an authoress in the year 1856, writing

> . . . with one hand for the booksellers
> While working with the other for myself,
> And Art . . .

And yet, Mrs. Browning's heroine cannot, in justice to the species, be considered a career woman at heart. It is true that she has 'clipt the curls before her eyes', but not for one moment does she cease to be self-conscious about her shorn state. She may scribble till midnight in her attic, review books, write a masterpiece and become famous, but all that makes her none the less ready to admit to Romney, whenever she is given a second chance, that

> . . . Art is much, but Love is more.
> O Art, my Art, thou'rt much, but Love is more!

It is difficult to feel that, by her defection, the structure of woman's employment lost one of its sturdier props.

Of quite another calibre is the strong-minded journalist drawn by Mrs. Lynn Linton, in *Sowing the Wind* (1867). Mrs. Linton, herself the first woman newspaper writer to receive a fixed salary, wrote from inside knowledge of newspaper offices; and although

by 1867 she was veering towards anti-feminism, and does not
make Jane Osborne her heroine, she does not hide her sympathy
for her. Her own first interview, in 1848, with the editor of the
Morning Chronicle, was undoubtedly used as material for *Sowing the Wind*.

'So! you are that little girl who has written that queer book and
want to be one of the press-gang, are you?' he said, half-smiling
and speaking in a jerky and unprepared manner, both singular and
reassuring.

I took him in his humour and smiled too.

'Yes, I am the woman,' I said.

'Woman, you call yourself? I call you a whipper-snapper,' he
answered good-humouredly.[17]

Such was the manner in which Miss Eliza Lynn received the
freedom of a newspaper office. Her bachelor girl, Jane Osborne,
is not, like many later feminists, caricatured out of credibility.
She was

a tall, bony girl of 21 or thereabouts . . . she was decidedly plain,
but she had fine grey eyes, large, deep-set and intelligent and a pro-
fusion of rich, auburn hair. Her skin was of a duck's egg white, fine
and soft, but covered with freckles; her nose was blunt and positive;
her lips wide, clumsy and ill-defined; her hands were small and good,
but her nails were dirty and her shoes were down at heel with the
stockings rumpled round the ankles.

Unlike most career women, she does not lower her colours, and
by the end of volume three she is still unmarried, still rejoicing
in her independence. About the employment of women, in
general, her editor has some pungent remarks to make.

'I say, Smith, how do you find this employment of women answers
in the office?'

'Pretty well, when they have common sense, which is not often,'
said Smith. 'Their two worst faults are looseness and partiality: and
their most annoying, the uncertainty of their work and their want of
reliable power. One day they do magnificently and you think you
have found a treasure; the next they send you in a dozen slips of
trash you cannot use . . . Then they are so desperately touchy! If
you pull them up for their faults and rap their knuckles as you would
a man's they fire up and stand on their dignity as ladies—the little
fools! The fact is the creatures want the cream of both states—the

independence and the money-getting power of men and the conventional respect of drawing room ladies; which is ridiculous, you know, and can't be done.'

'Then why do you have them?' asked Harvey.

'Why? Because they do better than men in some things. Their perceptions are finer—and because I pity them so much, poor creatures.'

While Jane is the forerunner of many similar bachelor girls in feminist history, she is a type seldom to be met with in the Victorian novel—a woman for whom it was the highest compliment to be treated like a man.

What we women want so much is that mixed knowledge got by men—the knowledge you pick up among each other at clubs and lectures and in places. You have such different friends—one is an artist, one a chemist, one an engineer and so on, and if you have brains you can keep yourselves informed of the last things in art, science and politics. But those of us who have any brains—and they are precious few!—get no help from one another except about babies and fashions according to the kind of thing the woman is . . . I'm proud of being on the press. I know I am proud of being able to do the work of a man among men.

Despite herself, Mrs. Linton cannot avoid showing Jane in a sympathetic light as she voices the unspoken thoughts of many women who, without rumpled stockings or dirty nails, were capable of feeling the same impatience with domesticity as Jane did. Aurora Leigh's artistic contempt of the tricks of the journalist's trade that forced her to learn the use

> Of the editorial 'we' in a review,
> As courtly ladies' the fine trick of trains

contrasts pleasingly with Jane's naïve enjoyment of her new power. Her confession to her sympathetic cousin, Isola, of the inner happiness her work has brought her, is strangely touching and provides a valuable glimpse into the mental processes of a thorough-going feminist of 1867.

'There is nothing purely feminine about me. I don't like babies; I despise obedient wives; I'd like to strangle the whole lot of curled and scented lady-killers, and I think love the veriest rubbish and moonshine in the world . . . And now I'm going to do what your soft women cannot do,' Jane said, with a certain accent of pride in her rough voice. 'I'm going to write a leader for a daily. Babies and love and the graces and prettiness are all very fine, I dare say, but give me the real solid pleasures of work—a man's work—work that influences the world—work that is power. To sit behind the scenes and pull the strings—to know that what one says as "We" in the "Comet" is taken among thinking men as a new gospel, when if you had said it as I, Jane Osborne, it would have been sneered at as woman's babble—to feel that strange thrill of secret, mental power—no, I would not give that up for all the happiness of your so-called womanly woman. You do not know the intense delight of such a life as mine . . . Poor, shabby, ugly, hard-worked, an absolute negation of all charms and all apparent pleasures—to look at there is nothing in me for anybody to envy—and yet, Isola, when I think of myself as one of the real, influential workers of the world—one of the uncatalogued movers of society and men's minds I feel as if I had found the treasure which you are all seeking.'

No such deep note is struck by Miss Yonge in *The Clever Woman of the Family* (1865), which is a studied parallel between two clever women—one, the Squire's daughter, Rachel, a progressive feminist, and the other, Ermine, an intellectual invalid. Rachel is allowed, in the end, to develop into an ideal wife and mother, but not before her feminist schemes have brought ridicule on her head. All the more prominent feminist activities of the day are heavily caricatured. Rachel is eloquent over the evils of the lace-making system ('everything was a "system" with Rachel'): she founds the F.U.E.E. (Female Union of Englishwomen's Employment), edits the Journal of Female Industry, but makes her first big mistake when she entrusts the running of her Industrial Home to a charlatan. Miss Yonge makes no attempt to put a delicate edge on her satire. When Rachel is unsuccessful in getting her contributions accepted by an intellectual paper, *The Traveller,* she decides to offer them to the *Englishwoman's Hobbyhorse.* Her light reading for the railway carriage is the Report of the Social Science Congress, and her travelling plans include a visit to Scotland to study the principle of diffused education, to Holland to see the Grand Reformatory for the Destitute, and to Switzerland to view the Hospital for Cretins.

It is quite clear that Ermine, on the other hand, fulfils Miss

6

Yonge's ideal of all that a clever woman should be as she lies
on her couch (an article of furniture no novel of Miss Yonge
was ever known to lack) and pens her learned essays on the
Edgeworth system of education, on the countryside, or on
matters scientific for *The Traveller's Review*. Her introduction
to the paper was effected in a womanly way through literary
friends of her brother, and, by her free-lance efforts, she helps
to support her sister and herself. Despite her erudition, she re-
tains her modest reserve—allied with the calm superiority of one
who, in a lady-like, recumbent position, can nevertheless beat
the feminists at their own game. To her faithful lover, who returns from India to join in the general chorus of admiration, she
is suitably unassuming on the subject.

'And now I am going to make you useful. The editor of *The
Traveller* is travelling and has left his work to me. Will you copy a
few letters for me? Here is some paper with the office stamp.'
'What an important woman you are, Ermine.'
'If you had been in England all this time you would see how easy
the step is into literary work.'

Although the struggle for women's medical degrees began in
1858, it was not resolved until 1877. And in that year Charles
Reade, in *A Woman-Hater*, gave a full, enthusiastic account of
the battle for the recognition of women doctors and presented to
the Victorian reading public their first woman doctor of fiction,
Dr. Rhoda Gale. Even before then there are, however, occasional
references in the novel to the possibility of women becoming
doctors—a possibility that the novelists found intriguing. One
of Rachel's foibles as the Clever Woman of the Family is to
practise medicine within her circle and to advocate reform without. And, despite the disastrous effect of her little globules, she
is listened to with apprehensive respect by her relatives.

'We must prevent the market from being drugged by diverting the
supply (of governesses) into new lines.'
'Are there any new lines?' asked Fanny, surprised at the progress
of society in her absence.
'Homeopathic doctresses,' whispered Grace.
'Why not—I ask, why not? Some women have broken through
prejudice and why should not others? Do you not agree with me

Fanny? that female medical men—I mean medical women—would
be an infinite boon?'
'It would be very nice if they would never be nervous.'
'Nerves are all a matter of training . . .'

Mrs. Brookfield, though in favour of higher education for
women, was not an advocate of medical training, and in *Not a
Heroine* (1873), she provides yet another young lady whom, from
her 'clump-soled, rough-looking boots', readers could discern
from afar off to be a feminist.

The well-trained Mrs. Scudamore shuddered as she heard Lavinia
discussing medical education for women with her husband—and
questioning him firmly as to his sensations on entering a dissecting
room for the first time. Upon this even the easy-going Sir Philip
Ogleby interposed, saying:
'My dear child, I can allow you to attend female suffrage meetings
and education lectures to any extent, but I shall certainly draw the
line if you take to dissection—it's nasty, I assure you it is.'
'I am not such a fool as to intend to do anything of the kind,'
Lavinia answered. 'It happens not to be my vocation, but as I have
the privilege of knowing more than one member of Mr. Scudamore's
profession who happen to be women I should like, as a mere outsider, to know how they have got over the difficulties which appear to
me to be the most trying in their most honourable career.'

'It happens not to be my vocation'—Lavinia's remark, which
falls so airily on modern ears, must in 1873 have seemed full of
heavy significance. For until recently marriage had been the only
profession that could be considered to deserve the title of vocation—wage-earning had been, at best, a stop-gap. But many
writers there were, who so objected to the idea, in general, of
careers for women that they never got down to condemning any
one career in particular. Trollope is an outstanding example of
this class of reactionary novelist; in *North America* (1862) he
had roundly stated his views.

This is the question of women's work; how far the work of the
world, which is now borne chiefly by men, should be thrown open to
women further than is now done . . . Where is the limit to be drawn
and who shall draw it? . . . A woman now could not well be a cab-
driver in London; but are these advocates sure that no woman will
be a cab-driver when success has attended their efforts? And would

they like to see a woman driving a cab? . . . Higher branches of work require study, apprenticeship, a devotion of youth: and that they will not give. It is very well for a young man to bind himself for four years, and to think of marrying four years after that apprenticeship is over, but such a prospectus will not do for a girl. While the sun shines the hay must be made, and her sun shines earlier in the day than that of him who is to be her husband . . . The object now sought is not of relieving distress . . . The idea is that women will ennoble themselves by making themselves independent, by working for their own bread instead of eating bread earned by men. It is not the woman who desires it but her philanthropical, philosophical friends who desire it for her . . . The best right a woman has is the right to a husband, and that is the right to which I would recommend every young woman to turn her best attention.

Such were the doctrines which Trollope thumped home in his novels, aided considerably by the charming way in which his heroines made their hay and claimed their rights. Mary, in *The Vicar of Bullhampton,* was voicing a sentiment common to all when she said to Walter: 'But you must think of yourself. For a woman after all, it doesn't matter much. She isn't expected to do anything particular. A man must look to his own career. . .'

It was still, indeed, only a brave heroine who would admit to the craving for a career—even if, as in a minor novel of 1870, *Which is the Heroine?*, she spends most of her time 'reading books and thinking' and longing for some obligatory work to fill her days. Miss Graham, while admitting that she has 'often envied City men that passed me in such a hurry with their papers under their arms or their little black bags in their hands, all intent on business, rushing along on foot or hailing an omnibus as if every moment was precious to them' eagerly denies her lover's accusations that she 'goes in for the rights of women'.

'Lord Montfort, what *do* you mean?' she answered in great trepidation. 'I never said that—I only said . . .' She paused, blushing crimson.

'That you wished to do things like men,' he answered quite gravely but with a twinkle of merriment in his eyes all the while.

'Oh, Lord Montfort, how *can* I explain to you that I never meant that? Will you believe me that I think women holding forth about their rights the most terrible things on earth.'

'We shan't have you taking out your degree as a doctor or a lawyer then, Miss Graham?'

'Oh no, *not for anything*,' she answered, with a look of genuine distress. 'I think a woman who steps out of her place should be despised by everyone; no one need respect her; let her leave those things to men who will always do them much better than she can and only laugh at her in the end for trying to compete with them: and very richly she will deserve that and everything else she gets for her pains . . .'

'Brava! Miss Graham. I like your enthusiasm.'[18]

It would not be unfair to the Career Woman in the mid-Victorian novel to end with this sharply italicised note of feminine horror ringing in our ears. The majority of novelists referred to in this chapter—as will have been noted—were women, and for the few writers that were willing to champion her cause there were vast numbers who entertained dark suspicions of her. As yet, too, only the outstanding professions, those requiring exceptional talent, had received the approval of novelists as worthy occupations for their heroines. But a beginning had been made and it was only a matter of time before the democratic doctrines regarding women and work, which from 1857 onwards were so sturdily upheld and widely circulated, made their full impact upon fiction. So that when we find—as we do, some twenty years later, in Grant Allen's novel—A Typewriter Girl composedly filling the role of novel-heroine we do well to remember that, without the efforts of the Langham Place feminists on her behalf, without the earlier recommendations from their Employment Bureau, she would never had been considered eligible for the position.

CHAPTER IV

The Rights of Women

1. A RAPTURE OF SUBMISSION

A PARTIALITY for good works, or even for good books, did not necessarily condemn the Victorian woman to solitary feminist footpaths. Far ahead of her, the indomitable figures of Miss Mary Carpenter and Miss Emily Davies might be visible, but as long as she picked her way with ladylike care, the worst that could be said of her was that she was 'progressive'. There was no such loophole, however, for the woman who concerned herself neither with good books nor with good works but with her legal rights. Victorians could find no excuse for her at all. She was the feminist proper, the real 'Women's Rights Woman', whose avowed aim was to turn society upside down and to get rid of the hallowed doctrine of sex-inequality. If she were allowed to get the upper hand, then the day would surely dawn when the most foolish of men would awaken to find himself, no longer by virtue of his sex, *ipso facto* superior to the most intelligent of women. And it was against the coming of that dreadful dawn that the Victorian age resolutely set its face.

In comparison with the other movements the drive for legal equality was late in getting under way. W. R. Greg, writing in 1868, commented:

WOMAN is the subject which for some time back our benevolence has been disposed to take in hand, fitfully and piecemeal. First it was the factory girls; then the distressed needlewomen; then aged and decayed governesses; latterly, Magdalens in esse or in futurum. The cry of 'Women's Rights' reached us chiefly from America and created only a faint echo here. WE have concerned ourselves more with 'Woman's Mission' and 'Woman's Employment'.[1]

But despite the stouter, earlier emancipated lungs on the other side of the Atlantic, the Rights of Women movement did, in England of the '60's, assume the form of an organised campaign.

Before then, individual protests had been entered with small success against the anomalies of women's legal position. As early as 1837 Caroline Norton was agitating on behalf of herself and others like her who, separated from their husbands, were denied all access to their children—and it was mainly through her efforts that two years' later the Infants' Custody Act* was passed. In 1854, Barbara Leigh Smith placed before the public for the first time full revelations, in pamphlet form and in simple language, of 'Laws relating to English Women'. With the result that English Women, who had never known till now the dangers they had passed, began to express some mild interest in their precarious legal position: an interest which the author indefatigably consolidated in a petition, bearing thousands of feminine signatures, to be presented in the Commons on behalf of a Married Women's Property Bill. Many of its supporters were happily married women like Mrs. Browning, Mrs. Howitt and Mrs. Jameson—or like Mrs. Gaskell, whose enthusiasm had not been marked: 'Though I don't see the definite end proposed by these petitions . . . I'll sign.' The bid failed, largely through the introduction of a counter-attraction in the form of a Marriage and Divorce Bill, but, although married women with property were destined to dangle their heels in Parliamentary stocks for the next thirty years, it was soon obvious that women were becoming increasingly knowledgeable about their legal drawbacks. In 1859, for instance, *The What-not* or *Ladies' Handy Book* saw personally to the enlightenment of the betrothed young lady upon the hard economic facts of her position.

It is probably not generally known that when once a woman has accepted an offer of marriage all she has or expects to have becomes virtually the property of the man she has accepted as her husband and no gift or deed executed by her is held to be valid; for were she permitted to give away or otherwise settle her property between the period of acceptance and the marriage he might be disappointed in the wealth he looked to in making an offer.

The feminists worked hard to accustom their sex to the idea that it was not unwomanly in a wife to feel a certain interest in

* The Infants Custody Act (1839) laid down that mothers against whom adultery had not been proved might have custody of their children under 7 and right of access to their older children.

her own property and, once they had succeeded so far, they did not let the matter drop. For the next ten years a stream of petitions from all classes flowed in upon Parliament. Document-signing became a new feminine accomplishment. Women who had never before appended their name to anything more significant than the butcher's order, now found a strangely flattering value set upon their signature. In 1869 Lady Amberley's journal records that, accompanied by her husband, she had been going the round of the cottages at Littleworth and had got '235 signatures—mainly women' to send up to the second reading of another Property Bill. But although, in 1870, some success was achieved, in that a working woman was given control of her own earnings, it was not until 1882 that a married woman was declared to be absolute mistress of her own property.

The Marriage and Divorce Act of 1857, which had jostled the Property Bill out of the limelight, was nominally in favour of women but served rather, by the inadequacy of its concessions, to bring the whole matter to public notice. Up till this time there had been no method of obtaining a divorce except by Act of Parliament, granted only on the application of the husband and founded on the adultery of the wife. By the 1857 Act, divorce was rendered less costly, by being made available through the law courts. But the wife could apply for divorce only if her husband were somewhat of a specialist in infidelity. Adultery, without variations on the theme, was not enough. If, however, he carried his sexual delinquencies to the point of committing incest, rendered himself liable to criminal prosecution, or coupled his adultery with legal cruelty or criminal desertion for two years and upwards, then the law had consolation for the injured wife. The *Westminster Review* condemned outright the measure as futile:

Specious excuses are sometimes advanced for this difference with regard to men and women. No man it is urged, in whom remains any sense of honour, could receive back to his embraces the violator of his marital confidence, but there are few cases in which an injured wife might not gracefully pardon an erring husband.[2]

The agitators had enough to do with the actual legal structure of marriage, however, without concerning themselves with the

movement towards a single moral standard. For marriage had
suddenly taken on an extraordinarily complicated appearance, as
the *Westminster Review* of 1864 pointed out:

The greatest social difficulty in England to-day is the relationship
between men and women. The principal difference between ourselves and our ancestors is that they took society as they found it
while we are self-conscious and perplexed. We see the difficulties and
dangers but we do not see the way out of them. The institution of
marriage might almost seem just now to be upon its trial . . .[3]

With the way prepared for it by the property and divorce
agitations, it was in the '60's that the trial of the institution of
marriage was really opened—when feminists demanded not only
full legal, but also political, equality, and led by the chief prose-
cutor, John Stuart Mill, probed darkly into man's base motives
for withholding their rights from them. The actual events of the
decade were unremarkable enough. In 1865, the same year as
Mill was elected to Parliament, a Ladies' Discussion Society was
formed; in 1866 Mill presented an unsuccessful suffrage petition
in the Commons; in 1867, the Woman's National Suffrage Society
was started and, in 1869, women were granted the municipal
franchise. Had feminists been content with the surface mechanics
of their campaign, its implications would have been far less
searching. But, as it was, a Ladies' Discussion Society could
scarcely be expected to concentrate upon anything as impersonal
as the vote when it was obvious to the least clear-thinking lady
among them that it was the whole relationship of the sexes that
was in need of adjustment. A ballot paper alone, they decided,
would not resolve the problem . . . And so it was that the Victorian marriage contract—so long exempt from all reproach—
found itself, uneasily, underneath the feminine microscope.

The lead in their discussions was, needless to say, taken by
Mill, whose *Subjection of Women*, though not published till
1869, had been drafted eight years earlier, and whose thoughts
and ideals were the common property of his disciples. It was a
new and heartening experience for feminists to feel the weight
of masculine backing and, more especially, the backing of a man
of international intellectual repute. Equally generous tributes to
women, equally sweeping demands for women had already been

made—but almost invariably, alas! by women. What was unusual in the *Subjection of Women* was not Mill's avowal of his belief in the complete equality of the sexes, although that indeed was encouraging, but the wholehearted trouncing he administered to the Victorian ideal of marriage. He concerned himself with the psychological effect of the supposed inferiority of women upon the whole marital relationship and upon the character of husband and wife, and swept into the attack with the observation, 'What is now called the nature of women is eminently artificial—the result of forced repression and unnatural stimulation.'

It is Mill's views, above all, which lie at the heart of the suffrage movement and which, more than any specific feminist achievement, made contemporary novelists realise that if they were to keep in tune with the times, their ideas of marriage and celibacy, and indeed of women as a whole, would have to undergo some sort of reassessment.

He pointed out that, because men had all the authority on their side—a legacy of the law of force which was almost everywhere abandoned as a ruling principle—few had any idea of the real characters, thoughts, feelings and capabilities of the women of their own families. The bad propensities of human nature were given full scope in the social institution of marriage. The power of the husband offered him licence for the indulgence of those points of his character he would repress in other relationships, and the subordination of the wife led her to depend upon feminine blandishments and influence for power. Her lack of personal freedom induced exaggerated self-abnegation. 'We are continually told that women are better than men by those who are opposed to treating them as if they were as good.' . . . In short, without equality, community of interests and likeness of intellects it was impossible to approach an ideal married state.

With these words and many more, Mill sought ruthlessly to ravish the Victorian marriage idyll. His conception of the right relationship of the sexes was obviously at a far remove from the popular viewpoint. Just how far, we may best assess by turning to three of the best-sellers of the 'forties and 'fifties—Thackeray, Dickens and Coventry Patmore—to see how they dealt with the subject.

Thackeray, in his dealings with his heroines, exhibits that

distinctive blend of clear-sightedness and sentimentality, of cynicism and mawkishness which has intrigued his critics for over a century. There are times when his young ladies seem as independent in their attitude to men and marriage as the most progressive of feminists. Laura Bell, for example, is capable of surveying the pampered Pen with disenchanted eyes, of rejecting with spirit his offensive proposal of marriage, the self-sacrifice of a 'broken man' of twenty-three:

'What have you got to give, Arthur?' Laura said, with grave sadness of tone . . . 'The next time, Arthur, when you offer yourself to a woman, do not say, as you have done to me, "I have no heart—I do not love you; but I am ready to marry you because my mother wishes for the match." We require more than this in return for our love—that is, I think so.'[4]

She is resentful of Pen's easy assumption of superiority, his selfishness and his indolence (it is with a 'bitter laugh' that Laura remarks, 'They are men, you know, and our superiors'); she is sensible of the difference between Warrington's admiration and 'Sultan Pen's yawning sovereignty and languid acceptance of homage'; she has a mind of her own and a sense of humour and her attachment to Pen is explained away by Thackeray, with ironic detachment reminiscent of Jane Austen: 'With whom shall a young lady fall in love but with the person she sees? . . . You have an instinct within you which inclines you to attach yourself to someone.'*

Much more advanced than Laura is Ethel Newcome, a charming spirited young woman, tall, dark, resolute, frank—not averse to the judicious use of slang. ' "Hit one of your own size, Barnes," says Miss Ethel (who had a number of school phrases from her little brothers and used them on occasion skilfully).' Her ideas about arranged marriages are modern and witty:

'I think, grandmamma,' Ethel said, 'we young ladies in the world, when we are exhibiting, ought to have little green tickets pinned on our backs with "Sold" written on them; it would prevent trouble and any future haggling, you know. Then at the end of the season the owner would come and carry us home.'[5]

* Cf., Captain Benwick in *Persuasion*.—'He had an affectionate heart. He must love somebody.'

But whenever the outlines of Ethel or Laura are in danger of becoming too well defined, they are blurred for the reader by the blanket of womanly devotion in which Thackeray huddles them. Again and again throughout the novels Thackeray interpolates such a passage as this (taken at random from *The Adventures of Philip*) with a chorus-like aspect and function: 'What have men done to get the love of some women? We don't earn it—we don't deserve it, perhaps. We don't return it. They bestow it on us . . . You are wonderful, women are! Your fidelities and ficklenesses alike marvellous.'

It was with many such a paean that Thackeray perpetuated the myth of wonderful woman and undeserving man, despite direct evidence in his novels to the contrary. Whenever Thackeray generalises about women the personality of his heroine is lost and her skilfully goffered individuality is ironed out to a smooth halo. No discerning reader is unaware, in the first instance, of the contrast between 'poor, little, blushing, burning, weeping Charlotte' and that 'stunner' Ethel, or between 'that dolt, Amelia' (as Miss Rigby roundly called her) and Laura, the Maypole with the 'monstrous red lips'. But as soon as Thackeray considers them—not as young women—but as candidates for his ideal state of matrimony (situated half-way between the harem and the shrine) they become virtually indistinguishable. Even Ethel, the 'giddy, worldly girl' is sobered, first into Aunt Ethel, with strong views on infant baptism and visiting the poor, and, only after this period of self-abnegation, into Ethel, the perfect wife and mother. The mere thought of a happy marriage was enough to tug at Thackeray's heart strings and to dim his keen vision: 'As for me, I look forward to a quiet life; a quiet little home, a quiet little library full of books, and a little Someone, *dulce ridentem, dulce loquentem*, on t'other side of the fire, as I scribble away at my papers.'[6]

Who is the little Someone? Certainly not Becky nor Beatrix, the heartless, witty and ambitious, whom Thackeray wisely made no attempt to fit into his Procrustean marriage bed, but equally certainly it could be any other of his young matrons. All true women, for Thackeray, have this duality. 'Angelic creatures'— 'sainted women'—whom men can bow down and worship, in the abstract, but who, in practice, compose their feathers happily

in their little domestic nests (the metaphor is a favourite of
Thackeray's) and, bright-eyed, sing the praises of the worldly-
wise male.

However humdrum Thackeray's conclusion about the marriage
relationship, the topic of Woman he found fascinating and enig-
matic. Not so Dickens. He was unshakably convinced of the
complete comprehensibility of all young women under the age
of five-and-twenty. His heroines, as in *David Copperfield*, tend
to fall into two main types (stature often being the decisive
factor): the tall, composed, steadfast and sensible, and the small,
fluttering, playful and dependent. In each case her appeal lies
through the graces and affections. A 'true and loving heart'—
Dickens demands no more for a happy marriage than that—
but also no less. It his *sine qua non*, his Midas touch, his pro-
prietary panacea. 'They were a tender-hearted, simple. foolish set
of women altogether.' What might be dispraise from another
author is a high tribute from Dickens. What matter though they
be small of wit, as long as they are great of heart? And yet,
despite their loving selflessness, the names of Dickens' women-
folk fall heavily on the ear as their long procession passes by—
Agnes Wickfield, Kate Nickleby, Florence Dombey, Esther Summerson, Little Dorrit, Sissy Jupe, Ruth Pinch, Little Em'ly, and
many more. They may be incandescent with virtue, but they do
not strike a responsive spark. Those who start out with some
individuality (or, more commonly, eccentricity), like Caddy
Jellyby or Loo Bounderby or Bella Wilfer, are in the end turned
out, like so many pale-pink blancmanges, in the same dutiful
mould. Dolly Vardon has a certain charm and several redeeming
faults, but only once, in all his novels, is Dickens startled out of
his normal, kindly, patronising attitude towards the Little
Woman into something like adult passion. The words of Pip
to Estella are those of a lover obsessed with the idea of one
woman, different from all others for him :

'You are part of my existence, part of myself. You have been in
every line I have ever read since I first came here, the rough common
boy whose poor heart you wounded even then. You have been in
every prospect I have ever seen since—on the river, on the sails of the
ships, on the marshes, in the clouds, in the light, in the darkness, in
the wind, in the woods, in the sea, in the streets. You have been the

embodiment of every graceful fancy that my mind has ever become acquainted with . . . Estella, to the last hour of my life, you cannot choose but remain part of my character, part of the little good in me, part of the evil.'[7]

But it is not often that a Dickens heroine is touched with poetry or given the heady taste of power. Haughtiness and vanity, cold-heartedness and pride in her self-sufficiency, these are not qualities to take into the prose of marriage, and it was only in a weak moment that Dickens consented to a last page metamorphosis. Estella, the star out of reach, has to be saddened and humbled, 'a different woman', before marriage can be contemplated. Ruth Pinch, busy at her beefsteak pudding—'Pleasant little Ruth! Cheerful, tidy, bustling, quiet little Ruth'—and not Estella, the capricious, is Dickens' more normal matrimonial ideal.

Perhaps most revealing of all mid-Victorian documents concerning the marriage relationship is *The Angel in the House*, that gentlemanly exaltation of wedded bliss which, written in 1854, had by 1860 become really popular. Patmore omitted nothing. Neither bridal, apprehensive innocence:

> O Muse who dost to me reveal
> The mystery of a woman's life,
> Relate how 'tis a maid might feel
> The night before she's crowned a wife!
> Lo, sleepless in her little bed
> She lies and counts the hours till noon
> Ere this tomorrow she'll be wed,
> Ere this? Alas, how strangely soon!
> A fearful blank of ignorance
> Lies manifest across her way . . .

Nor wifely modesty:

> . . . veils are due
> To woman's feelings . . .
> I did not call you Dear or Love
> I think till after Frank was born.

Nor joyful inferiority:

> A rapture of submission lifts
> Her life into celestial rest, . . .

> And all the wisdom that she has
> Is to love him for being wise.

Nor, above all, the importance of her calling:

> He discommended girl-hood. What
> For sweetness like the ten years wife,
> Whose customary love is not
> Her passion or her play but life.

It was small wonder, therefore, in view of the sentiments expressed so admirably in *The Angel in the House*, that many women became speechless as they pondered the impertinence of Mill's solicitude. Some others, like Catherine Winkworth, chose to find it amusing.* But, to a happy few, it must have been as if sunshine from the outside world of men were, for the first time, striking through the Venetian blinds and heavy velvet curtains that draped their shrines and making their domestic fires flicker pale in apprehension.

It can be fairly said that the movement for rectifying the palpable injuries inflicted on women by law met with conditional public approval; that for full, legal and political equality met with very little encouragement at all. The suffrage movement of the sixties was too intent on upsetting the *status quo*, on putting dangerous ideas into the heads of wives who had hitherto been content to have no ideas at all, to be condoned on humanitarian grounds. Victorians, as a whole, adopted the fashionable Benthamist outlook on the question of suffrage; if ninety-nine women were happy without the vote and one unhappy, then it was very sad indeed for the one, but there was no possible justification for embarrassing the others by inflicting on them rights and privileges they had no desire to use. Nobody, on the other hand, need be particularly feminist to be willing to espouse the cause of the genuinely injured wife, who was reminiscent in many ways of the distressed milliner or factory girl of former years.

But, while the public was not reluctant to shake its head over the sordid revelations that accompanied the Married Women's

* 'I am reading Mill on the *Subjection of Women* and learning from it with some amusement what wretchedly oppressed, miserable creatures we all are—especially you unfortunate married women.' (Letter of June 16, 1869.)

Property and Divorce agitations—disclosures of drunken husbands, abandoned wives, neglected children—novelists remained aloof from such unsavoury externals and suspended their interest until the 'trial of the institution of marriage', of the '60's, brought more equivocal issues to light. The frequent compassionate references in the earlier novels to the need for fairer legal treatment of women are, in the main, passing allusions. It was, after all, the basic, happy, marriage relationship, the ideal state of wifely submission and dependence that had so long formed the stuff of his novel, with which the average writer was concerned, and it was not until that state was called into question that the Rights of Women campaign can be said to show signs of exerting any centripetal influence upon the novel. From that time on, however, it became increasingly difficult to ignore the existence of a new, critical and importunate attitude towards marriage, and it was only the insensitive novelist who could remain unaffected by it and continue to look upon the marriage state as something which could be taken completely for granted.

2. LIKENESS OF INTELLECTS

There is some social interest in those novels of the '50's which were affected, however superficially, by the contemporary agitations for legal reform. In 1848, nine years before the Divorce Act, in all its inadequacy, was passed, Kingsley numbered, in *Yeast*, among the degradations suffered by the working classes, the cruelties of the existing divorce laws:

'Good God! Is there no escape for her from that tyrant?'
'No, Sir, it's only you gentlefolks who can afford such luxuries. Your poor man may be tied to a harlot or your poor woman to a ruffian, but once done, done for ever.'
'Well,' thought Lancelot, 'we English have a characteristic way of proving the holiness of the marriage tie. The angel of justice and pity cannot sever it—only the stronger demon of money.'*

Dickens put the case even more pungently, though from the masculine viewpoint, in *Hard Times* (1854), in which one of the main characters, Stephen Blackpool, is shown struggling im-

* According to a contemporary calculation, the cost of invoking an Act of Parliament for a divorce was from £800-£1,000.

potently after eighteen years of suffering, to release himself from
the stranglehold of a drunken, demented travesty of a wife. The
conclusion that Stephen wearily comes to is that it is 'fro' first
to last a muddle'—but less of a muddle for richer people who

'. . . are not bonded together for better, for worst so fast, but that
they can be set free fro' their misfortnet marriages, and marry ower
agen. When they dunnot agree, for that their tempers are ill assorted,
they ha' rooms o' one kind an' another in their houses, above a bit,
and they can live asunders. We folk ha' only one room, and we can't.
When that won't do they ha' gowd an' other cash, an' they can say,
"This for yo' an' that for me", an' they can go their separate ways. We
can't. Spite o' all that, they can be set free for smaller wrongs than
mine. So, I mun be ridden o' this woman, and I want to know how?'
    'No how,' returned Mr. Bounderby.
    'If I do her any hurt, sir, there's a law to punish me?'
    'Of course there is.'
    'If I flee from her, there's a law to punish me?'
    'Of course there is.'
    'If I marry t'other dear lass, there's a law to punish me?'
    'Of course there is.' . . .
    'Now, a' God's name,' said Stephen Blackpool, 'show me the law to
help me!'

But as divorce was then possible, even for the richer classes,
only by attaching the stigma of adultery to the wife, a *divorcée*
was one of the facts of life from which a young lady obediently
averted her eyes. Thackeray, in *The Newcomes*, painted a sombre
picture of the fate of Lady Clara Pulleyn, after she has been
driven to the arms of her former suitor, Lord Highgate, by the
insupportable cruelty of Barnes Newcome, her husband:

The very man who loves her and gives her asylum, pities and de-
plores her . . . All the sisterhood of friendship is cut off from her . . .
She knows she has darkened the lot and made wretched the home of
the man whom she loves best . . . In the country lanes or the streets
of the county town, neighbours look aside as the carriage passes in
which she sits, wretched and lonely . . . No wonder that her husband does not like home except for a short while in the hunting
season. No wonder that he is away all day; how can he like a home
which she has made so wretched?

Clara's fate is pitiful, but it is the lot of the runaway wife, and

7

Thackeray's wrath is directed only incidentally against the injustice of the divorce laws which allowed the husband enormous damages for 'having trampled on the poor, weak young thing and scorned her and driven her to ruin'. His main quarrel is with the parents who are the cause of such a tragedy, in that they sacrifice their children on the altar of a fashionable marriage. Thackeray is involved in the emotional situation rather than in legal reform. Unlike the middle-aged hero of a very minor novel of 1856, *The Gilberts and their Guests*, who states in formal terms the case for a change in the divorce laws:

'There is something deplorably at fault, Margaret, in the moral treatment which cases of this unfortunate description receive at the hands of society; the day must come when they will be more wisely dealt with.'

'You would not have them go unpunished?'

'I would, at least, not have all the punishment fall on one side and that the weakest,' replied Surrey.

'I confess I am of the opinion that it had best remain as it is,' said Mrs. Gilbert, 'marriage cannot be regarded in too sacred a light.'

'True, but it's being rendered more easily dissoluble by law would, I believe, rather rivet than loosen the true nature of such a bond.'[8]

By the time *East Lynne* was written, divorce was sufficiently in the air to embolden Mrs. Wood not only to make her heroine an erring wife and subsequent *divorcée*, but to show a clear partiality for the Lady Isabel that she denied the less interesting but blameless second wife. The *Englishwomen's Journal* of 1861, ever embarrassingly eager to tune into and transmit even the faintest of feminist thought-waves, commented: 'We cannot help thinking that the theme was suggested to her mind by reflexions on the practical results of the new Divorce Bill.' Be that as it may, few heroines can ever have suffered as Lady Isabel had to suffer to redeem herself in the public's eyes. To justify her own weakness for a technically wicked woman, Mrs. Wood relentlessly made her work her passage through desertion, disfigurement and poverty to her incognito situation, as governess to her own children in her husband's new ménage. When death finally came, it eased a strain that was fast becoming intolerable—a strain not only on the Lady Isabel but upon Victorian hearts and handkerchiefs. Everyone, from the Prince

of Wales* down, took a personal interest in Lady Isabel's fate.
But although both reader and heroine emerged, purified, from
the best-selling catharsis that was *East Lynne*, it is doubtful
whether the novel was likely to have purged the reader also of
anti-feminist prejudices. In spite of the hopeful attitude of the
Englishwomen's Journal and the kindly encouragement held out
by Mrs. Wood of ultimate forgiveness, even for a *divorcée*, in
death, it would show disregard of the *mot juste* to describe East
Lynne as thorough-going feminist fiction. Had Mrs. Wood, instead, chosen to lead an erring husband the hard route of
repentance, the situation would, of course, have held very different and fascinating possibilities.

It was not to be expected that authors, who had personal experience of legal injustices, would keep silent on the subject in
their novels. Mrs. Norton, an injured wife and mother, had
several hard things to say, in *Lost and Saved*, on the framing of
laws by men, for men. And Rosina Bulwer Lytton, whose sense
of injury grew with each passing year of separation from her
husband, let herself go in *Very Successful* (1856) on the somewhat arid topic of married women's property.

Mrs. Pemble had had no settlements made on her and was thus
left entirely at her husband's mercy and had nothing to trust to but
his honour. Poor, poor woman!

Alas! my young lady friends, it should at least be part of your
education to know that, notwithstanding the much vaunted British
constitution, it does not contain a single law for the redress or protection of married women—unless, indeed, they be the possessors of
large property stringently tied up upon themselves.

Neither Rosina's gibes nor Kingsley's muscular indignation
go very deep, however. It is in the next decade that we find
moral issues and underlying ideals of marriage exercising the
minds of even the more conservative writers. It is probably in
a poem—Meredith's *Modern Love* (1862)—that we find the most
adult and subtle conception of the marriage relationship. He
treats it as an affair of absolute emotional equality, in the success
or failure of which both husband and wife are equally involved.

* The Prince of Wales, while in Egypt, refused to join an expedi-
tion to view some troops—preferring to stay in his tent, smoking and
reading *East Lynne*.

There could be no more piquant contrast between two mid-Victorian poems than between *The Angel in the House* and *Modern Love*. The virginal expectation of the bliss of matrimony:

> Lo, sleepless in her little bed
> She lies and counts the hours till noon.

has been followed by the 'vain regret' of Meredith's marriage bed:

> By this he knew she wept with waking eyes:
> That, at his hand's light quiver by her head,
> The strange low sobs that shook their common bed,
> Were called into her with a sharp surprise,
> And strangled mute, like little gaping snakes,
> Dreadfully venomous to him . . .

For complacency and patronage, innocence and reverence, Meredith substitutes a love grown cold yet still aflame with torment, heart-searching and jealousy, intellectual analysis and painful honesty. Certainly no feminist would have claimed *Modern Love* as a testimonial for wedded equality. It is the story of a marriage which has failed, of unfaithfulness, of obsessive unhappiness—in short, of incompatibility of temperament, the modern catch-phrase which had no meaning for the staunch Victorian. But although, to some extent, they have been brought to this pass by their attempt at intellectual comprehension, instead of emotional apprehension, of their relationship, nevertheless the husband, conscious of the lack of dispassionate reasoning in his wife, baffled by the blend of the rational and instinctive in women, makes his plea, not for less brainpower, but more:

> Their sense is with their senses all mixed in,
> Destroyed by subtleties these women are!
> More brain, O Lord, more brain!

And although their union is severed, the ideal of equality remains whole and unharmed. The husband apportions the blame equally and without rancour:

> . . . I see no sin:
> The wrong is mixed. In tragic life, God wot,
> No villain need be! Passions spin the plot;
> We are betrayed by what is false within.

Most of the reviewers took up a high moral tone, considering the poem as a defamation and distortion of the fair face of matrimony. As usual, too, Meredith's indecision, his rooted disinclination to 'come out strong' ethically, irked them enormously—and *Modern Love* remained in obscurity for many years, until it found a public more disposed to appreciate its poetic truth. But other, more straightforward, issues concerning marriage were on the stocks. Mill's assertion, for instance, that the husband's right to dominate his wife led to tyranny, on one side, and hypocrisy, on the other, was substantiated at three-volume length by Mrs. Lynn Linton in *Sowing the Wind* (1867).

In this novel, the recurring question is the extent to which a wife should fulfil her marriage vow of obedience in matters affecting her own conscience. The heroine, Isola, is shown as striving, after five years of marriage, to expand her personality and to release herself from suffocating dependence on her husband's bounty. She does not pretend to legal equality but merely to the right to govern her own actions, to cultivate new interests and acquaintances, to make her own moral decisions—a right denied her by her husband, St. John, who firmly assures her that women should be ciphers—'ciphers that men alone can give a value to'. In the conflict that follows, feminine fibre triumphs and it is St. John who cracks first, under the strain of watching his wife disprove his cipher system a little more conclusively each day, and yields finally to madness and death. Once he has departed, his exhausted, though resilient, widow is allowed to find happiness with one more worthy to be her companion in life, one whom Mrs. Linton does not blush to describe as a 'true-hearted, leonine, granitic type' of man. But, while coping with her temperamental husband, Isola searches her soul, painfully and often, in an attempt to resolve her mental turmoil:

What would she do? He was her husband truly and she therefore owed him obedience; but had she no sense of right herself? Was the better thing of no account? And ought she to commit a baseness, as it seemed to her, merely out of a cowardly fear and to keep him in a good humour? Was it right to give up a moral principle simply to please even a husband? . . . These thoughts touched the unsolved problem of married life and uncovered the cancerous sore of home—namely, the right of the woman to independent moral action in opposition to her husband's will—her duty to God, as represented by her conscience, or her duty to the social law, as represented by her wifely submission.

Isola, clearly Mrs. Linton's idea of a perfect wife, is contrasted to her advantage with both an Amazon bachelor-girl and a Grizelda wife—but it is against the latter that the author directs her sharpest satire:

It was Mrs. Joyce's firm belief that all unhappy marriages dated from the wife only and that to the coldness, the independence and the want of the adoring faculty generally in women was due the sole cause of matrimonial disagreement. She was certainly very bitter to unhappy wives. Why were they not happy? she used to say pettishly. She was happy with her Timmy, why could not others do as she did? If men were cross, it was the woman's duty to be kind; if they were a little tyrannical, women should submit; she had no patience with this new doctrine of individuality and freedom and all such nonsense . . .

It was not so many years since Mrs. Joyce's attitude would have been considered no jesting matter; and although Mrs. Linton herself gave this 'new doctrine of individuality and freedom' only her qualified approval, she was sufficiently influenced by it to condemn outright the exploitation of docility by wives to gain their own ends.

'The real mistress,' said St. John hastily, 'is the most submissive wife.'
'Well, I would rather not have my own way if I had to get it by pretended submission,' said Isola warmly. 'I do not like that kind of thing at all. Far better to be honest and straightforward and to say out boldly what one wishes than to succeed by pretending an obedience which is in reality only manœuvring.'

It is an indication of how firmly established the idea of wifely submission was in Victorian minds that both St. John and another masterful husband, in a Trollope novel about the same time, were considered more likely to lose their reason than to compromise on such a point. In *He Knew He Was Right*, Trollope, for once dabbling in psychological preserves, verged on the melodramatic in his characterisation of a possessive husband. Trevelyan is so fond of dominating his wife that when she refuses to submit to his ruling in one particular matter, he broods,

exaggerates her obstinacy into infidelity, becomes mentally un-
hinged and is a raving lunatic by the end of volume three. The
point at issue is whether or not his wife should continue to
receive the afternoon calls of a man, who has a certain claim
upon her as an old friend of her father's but whom Trevelyan
knows to be an unrepentant old *roué*. He knows that he can
trust his wife implicitly but becomes obsessed with the notion of
forcing her into admitting that she has been in the wrong. While
she, drawing a firm if arbitrary line between obedience and submission, declares herself to be quite willing to obey her husband's
commands but just as unprepared to accept guilt merely to keep
the peace. Trollope makes it clear that his sympathies are with
her, that, notwithstanding the consequences and her initial obstinacy, she has in his opinion acted with spirit and integrity in
refusing to become a Griselda for her husband. My Lady
Griselda, of late, indeed had fallen strangely out of favour with
the novelist who seldom mentioned her name without a sneer.

And yet, although Trollope is on the wife's side, he does not
slur over the fact that, in any such separation as took place between the Trevelyans, it was the woman that suffered most—the
woman who was automatically judged by the Mrs. Joyces of her
sex to be in the wrong, who could not go out into the world by
herself, who, even although her husband was on the verge of
lunacy, could not claim the custody of her child from him. In
this novel, Trollope makes no demands of society on behalf of
wronged wives, as he does in *The Vicar of Bullhampton* on behalf of fallen women. He contents himself with giving a study of
a marriage wrecked by a wife, who not only knew that her husband was wrong, but did not exert herself to keep that knowledge
from him. And that the cautious Trollope chose to condone her
behaviour may be taken as fairly reliable evidence that the day
of the wife with the extinguished personality was inexorably
approaching its twilight hour.

The day of the wife with the expanding intellect, on the other
hand, was just dawning. No marriage, according to John Stuart
Mill, could be ideal without likeness of intellects, and for some
time now it had been accepted as advisable that a wife, with her
inferior advantages, should make a resolute attempt to educate
herself up to companion-standard at least. Even Dickens, that

Victorian internal combustion engine, who, by a system of prudent retarding, always contrived it so that his explosions occurred at the top dead centre of public opinion, was quite willing to have his little woman playfully attempt to ape her superior. His thumb-nail sketch in *Our Mutual Friend* (1865) of Mrs. John Harmon (*née* Bella Wilfer) as she pursues her wifely duties, gives some idea of how far he was prepared to go in this matter of equal intellects.

She always walked with him to the railroad and was always there again to meet him; her old coquettish ways a little sobered down (but not much) and her dress as daintily managed as if she managed nothing else. But . . . the dress would be laid aside, trim little wrappers and aprons would be substituted and Bella, putting back her hair with both hands as if she were making the most business-like arrangements for going dramatically distracted, would enter on the household affairs of the day. Such weighing and mixing, and chopping and grating, such dusting and washing and polishing, such snipping and weeding and trowelling and other small gardening, such making and mending and folding and airing, such diverse arrangements and above all such severe study. For she was under the constant necessity of referring for advice and support to a sage volume entitled the *Complete British Family Housewife* which she would sit consulting with her elbows on the table and her temples on her hands like some perplexed enchantress, poring over the Black Art.

Another branch of study claimed her attention for a regular period each day. This was the mastering of the newspaper so that she could be close up with John on general topics when John came home. In her desire to be in all things his companion she would have set herself with equal zeal to master Algebra or Euclid if he had divided his soul between her and either.

Miss Bella Wilfer behind a newspaper was one thing. A wife who surpassed or even equalled her husband in intellectual capacity quite another. She is not to be found in Dickens. Nor indeed among any of Trollope's heroines, quick-witted though they are as a family. And yet, outside of fiction, there were plenty of women, who, without any feminist sympathies, were fully aware of their mental superiority to men in their circle. Such, for instance, was Anne Thackeray, who, putting pen to paper, in 1859, relieved her feelings in a rush of indignation:

I talked to Mr. Mosely and Mr. Harcourt said aggravating things about women as usual. It's absurd to be annoyed as it's only a joke, but it's very riling. O ye heavens! Look at him and then look at me! Why am I to be contemptible all my days long . . . Why is he to be so much more worth in his own, in everybody else's estimation? Why has he got work and leisure and strength and height and a thousand more advantages which I can't get at, not if I try till I burst like the frog in the fable. Why am I ridiculous when I spar at him with foolish little thrusts? I'm sure my brains are as good as his. I could feel this last night when I was listening to his talk with Mr. Brook-field.[9]

Miss Thackeray, later Lady Ritchie, had never to contend, as far as we know, with the more intimate problem that confronted Miss Brontë—that of being sought in marriage by a man of lesser intellect. The latter in conversation on this topic with Mrs. Gaskell and Miss Winkworth, in 1851, expressed her grave concern.

'But, Katie, it has cost me a great deal to come to this . . . I cannot conceal from myself that he is *not* intellectual; there are many places into which he could not follow me intellectually . . . I do believe Mr. Nicholls is as reliable as you say, or I wouldn't marry him . . . Still, such a character would be far less amusing and interesting than a more impulsive and fickle one; it might be dull!'
'Yes, indeed,' said Lily (Mrs. Gaskell).
'For a day's companion, yes,' I said, 'but not for a life's . . . besides such a character would have the advantage that one might do the fickleness required one's self, which would be a relief sometimes.'
'Oh, Katie, if *I* had ever said such a wicked thing,' cried Lily; and then Miss Brontë . . .
'Oh, there is truth in it; so much so that I don't think *I* could ever have been so candid.'[10]

Mr. Nicholls has not placed on record any parallel conversation between himself and a couple of curate friends on the advisability of taking to himself a wife who would for ever be disappearing into many places where he 'could not follow her intellectually'. It was perhaps fortunate for the marriage rate that all Victorian suitors were not subjected to pre-marital examination by such stern critics; although, on the whole, it cannot be said that feminists' claims were excessive, in this matter of relative brainpower. It was a favourite, and disarming, feminist argument that, as no one could deny that the best feminine brains must, at least, be superior to the worst masculine ones, wide generalisations about the inferiority of woman's intellect could not be valid. And, although wives of good sound intellect become increasingly common in the novel as the higher education movement gained ground, it is only here and there that we come upon examples, in fiction, of the Mr. and Mrs. Nicholls' *ménage*, in fact.

A modified parallel, however, is provided in 1859 by Charles Reade who, always ebulliently eager to give woman her due, mates a female Chesterfield with a simple sailor. His heroine, Lucy Fountain, beautiful, tactful, and Machiavellian, gracefully allows herself to be converted into Mrs. David Dodd, for reasons which she states with appealing candour:

'To leave this interesting topic for a while,' said Lucy languidly, 'let me consult you, Miss Dodd. I have not, as you may have noticed, great abilities, but I have received an excellent education. To say nothing of these soi-disant accomplishments, with which we adorn and sometimes weary society, my dear mother had me well grounded in languages and history . . . I feel'—here she bit her lip—'myself fit for public life . . . I am ambitious . . .'

'Oh, you are, are you?'

'Very; and perhaps you will kindly tell me how I had best direct that ambition; the army?—no. Your brother's profession?—not for the world. Shall I lower my pretensions to the learned professions?'

'I don't doubt your cleverness—but the learned professions?'

'A woman has a tongue, you know, and that is their grand requisite.'

'I suppose you are making fun of me,' said Eve, 'but there is many a true word spoken in jest. You could be a better lawyer, parson or doctor than nine out of ten but they won't let us; they know we could beat them into fits at anything but brute strength and wickedness. So they have shut all those doors in us poor girls' faces.'

'There, you see,' said Lucy archly, 'but two lines are open to our honourable ambition—marriage and—watercolours. I think marriage the more honourable of the two; above all—it is the more fashionable. Can you blame me then if my ambition chooses the altar and not the easel?'[11]

It is quite obvious that the Dodd-Fountain union is destined for success and that there will be no point of conflict between Mr.

and Mrs. Dodd; when a female Chesterfield has made up her mind to make a career out of marriage she is capable of making even her superiority of intellect attractive to her husband. But indeed, there were few husbands who objected to their wives possessing brains. It was when their wives were found to be capable of putting those brains to good account, of specialising in their own particular branch of study, or even of earning money, that their forbearance was tried. Some husbands, like Mr. Gaskell, appeared to bear up under their wives' celebrity very philosophically—'William has composedly buttoned up the £10 they sent me for *Lizzie Leigh* in his pocket'; others may well have resented their position keenly. It is the second, more dramatic, possibility with which a minor novel of 1869, *Nigel Bartram's Ideal,* concerns itself—in only one volume, instead of the more normal three—but one volume of considerable interest.

In this novel, a gallant attempt is made to face the issue of whether mutual respect and loving companionship are possible between husband and wife, even when the balance of intellect is on the wife's side. Nigel Bartram is convinced that his wife, Marian, conforms to his negative ideal of womanhood—an ideal of 'quiet intelligence and sweet sincerity'—until he finds out that she is the author of a best-seller sensation novel called *Mark's Secret*. The discovery that she is much more celebrated, as an author, than he will ever be as a book-reviewer, gives him an unkind jolt and estrangement follows. There is, however, no easy way out down the path of tottering reason provided for Nigel Bartram as there was for Mrs. Linton's and Trollope's disappointed husbands. At first, it is true, he indulges his resentment at her superior abilities, very freely, upon his unfortunate wife:

'There must always be a certain superiority in a man's mind to a woman's, let the "women's rights" people say what they will,' she began with a faint smile.
'A very ingenious evasion!' he interrupted impatiently. 'But putting aside that, which is quite another question, you will allow, I suppose, that you are much cleverer for a woman than I for a man?'
She hung her head as if beneath a dire accusation.
'I have just one special talent,' she faltered deprecatingly.
'Marian!' he exclaimed, 'don't torment me with this absurd humility.'[12]

Soon, however, on looking back, Nigel finds that his old ideal seems somewhat savourless and uninteresting, after living with a wife to whom he gloomily persists in referring as 'a genius'. 'Out of the ruins of Nigel's old glad trustful belief in her there was growing up a new respect—a cold feeling perhaps for a husband, the sort of one an outsider might have had, but yet better than the hasty contempt and wrath that had followed on the discovery of his mistake.' [13] And once he has searched his heart sufficiently he decides, not only that his resentment is indefensible, but that his new love for Marian is now deeper and less patronising. A conversation with a broad-minded colleague conveniently clears his mind of its last lingering doubts:

'Why not let her write? I can't understand you at all. Are you jealous? Don't you want to be known as "the clever Mrs. Bartram's husband"? It does make rather a secondary personage of a man, but somehow I gave you credit for being too generous minded to care for that.'

'I don't know,' said Nigel honestly. 'I believe you have put into words a feeling that has rather bothered me and may have influenced me more than I supposed. I am not sure that we men ever *quite* like to feel ourselves inferior to our wives in anything but goodness. We believe, and we like to believe, that they are purer and better than we are, but I don't think we altogether wish them to be cleverer—more capable.' [14]

It is very seldom, in the mid-Victorian novel, that the problem of a wife with greater mental abilities is so squarely considered and it is not surprising that the author should have been a woman. Although it may seen a simple solution that the husband should gracefully accept and grow to relish his subsidiary role, it is not one that would have appealed to many male writers. The influence of a wife over her husband had never been denied but it was only occasionally suggested that, unless the wife were of equal mental stature with her husband, that same influence, by its very negative quality might tend to divert or even dry up the course of her husband's ambitions and energies. A vague suspicion was, however, making itself felt that a loving wife, a domestic atmosphere, the ties and responsibilities of home were not always enough in themselves to stimulate a man to his highest endeavours—Felix Holt, as a bachelor, naturally has well-formulated views on the inadvisability of marriage for an idealistic man:

'I'll never marry though I should have to live on turnips to subdue my flesh. I'll never look back and say, "I had a fine purpose once—I meant to keep my hands clean and my soul upright and to look truth in the face, but pray excuse me—I have a wife and children—I must lie and simper a little else they'll starve." '[15]

It is not only the restrictions imposed by the material conditions of marriage that Felix condemns. He is also fully convinced of the disastrous effect that marriage can have upon a man when he is mated with one who is educated neither to follow his mental excursions nor his spiritual quests. It is a problem that recurs again and again in the novels of George Eliot, most memorably perhaps, in the relationship of Rosamond and Lydgate. To Esther, Felix says:

'I can't bear to see you going the way of the foolish women who spoil men's lives. That's what makes women a curse; all life is stunted to suit their littleness . . . I wonder whether the subtle measuring of forces will ever come to measuring the force there would be in one beautiful woman whose mind was as noble as her face was beautiful —who made a man's passion for her rush in one current with all the great aims of his life.'

'A woman can hardly ever choose in that way,' said Esther, 'she is dependent on what happens to her. She must take meaner things because only meaner things are within her reach.'

George Eliot was fully aware that, however absorbing marriage might be for most women, there were always a few to whom the domesticities and endless small change of marriage might seem the 'meaner things' after a time. It was with the early days of marriage that most novelists concerned themselves, when love had not had time to grow weary, nor children to grow up—not with the middle watch of matrimony when any woman who had no other interests than her home and family found time hanging heavily on her hands. Mrs. Transome in *Felix Holt* is a shrewd sketch of just such a woman.

A little daily embroidery had been a constant element in Mrs. Transome's life; that soothing occupation of taking stitches to produce what neither she nor anyone else wanted, was then the resource of many a well-born and unhappy woman . . . It is a fact perhaps kept a little too much in the background, that mothers have a self larger than their maternity, and that when their sons have become taller than themselves, and are gone from them to college or into the world, there are wide spaces of their time which are not filled with praying for their boys, reading old letters and envying yet blessing those who are attending to their shirt buttons. Mrs. Transome was certainly not one of those bland, adoring, and gently tearful women. After sharing the common dream that when a beautiful man-child was born to her, her cup of happiness would be full, she had travelled through long years apart from that child to find herself at last in the presence of a son of whom she was afraid, who was utterly unmanageable by her and to whose sentiments in any given case she possessed no key.

George Eliot was, as usual, in the advance guard in her opinions. Mrs. Pendennis, who spent all her spare moments in putting up a prayer for young Arthur, had unquestionably far more sympathisers among Victorian readers than Mrs. Transome. But although Dickens' and Thackeray's appeal was as strong as ever and a novel like *The Semi-Attached Couple*, with its 1830 setting, attracted a large public mainly because of its uneventful character and its atmosphere of warm domestic stability, nevertheless, by the late sixties, placid family life was not all that Victorians expected of an ideal marriage. Something more they demanded—and Trollope was the author who gave it them. It was difficult to pin down exactly what that something was. It may have been the reverence with which he approached the subject of marriage, the importance he ascribed to it, that elevated it from a hum-drum relationship to the level of a rite. Certainly no other author went into the matter with such an infinity of unflagging interest. Some readers found the topic inclined to pall after a little; Trollope himself, never. An article in the *Fortnightly Review* of 1869 comments:

Then again we admit Mr. Trollope's power in describing young ladies in love and in doubt. He knows English girls by heart . . . But surely English ladies suffer occasionally other agony than doubts as to whether this or that lover is to be the man thrown over, accepted, snubbed, encouraged or drawn on. We say not a word against love in stories—but there are deep chords in woman's nature that this kind of love does not touch and as the prose laureate of English girls of the better class why should not Mr. Trollope record something else beside flirtations that end well?[16]

Here we find the feminist argument, once more, of 'deep chords in a women's nature' that marriage would not satisfy—but it is a blunt weapon to use against Trollope. For to his mind there could be nothing more important, more valuable for a woman than a flirtation that ended well. It was by marriage, and by marriage only, that women could exercise their supremacy, and he considered that only by sublimation of herself through her husband and children could a woman ever bring her full powers of influence for good into action. As far as he knew, there were no deep chords in women that a judicious marriage would not bring into harmony with life . . . And yet, despite Trollope's determined anti-feminism, his own ideal of marriage, if it does not include equality, is found, on examination, not to fall far short of Mill's other demands of 'community of interests and likeness of intellects'. It is true that he granted his heroines far more freedom in their virgin state than under the marriage yoke. But, practically without exception, they take with them into marriage intelligence, self-sufficiency and a certain proud consciousness of their own value which makes them reluctant to demand that which should be theirs by right.

Trollope's unrivalled popularity as high-priest of marriage, in fiction, was not so much because his treatment of the subject was more adult and sane than that of Dickens but because his heroines are shown to be worthy in every way of challenging masculine respect and yet prefer, instead of entering into the lists with their men, to offer them their joyful allegiance. It was on reading Trollope that Victorians must have felt their ideal of wifely submission was in its finest hour. No Trollope heroine, for instance, would embark on marriage like Elizabeth Bennet, prepared to love, but also discreetly to laugh at, her husband for his own good; once she has chosen a man whom she considers worthy of controlling her actions she is more than content to abide by his judgement. There is, furthermore, never any question of a *quid pro quo* where gallivanting husbands are concerned. Though Fanny Robarts is spirited enough to rebuke her absentee Frank, she is very ready to receive him back without further reproaches, while the treatment meted out to Harry in *The Claverings*, when he returns to his *fiancée* after engaging himself to another woman, must have made painful reading for a militant feminist.

The tact of women excels the skill of men, and so perfect was the tact of these women that not a word was said which wounded Harry's ear. He had come again into their fold and they were rejoiced and showed their joy. He who had gone astray had repented and they were beautifully tender to a repentant sheep.[17]

It was from the danger of making a mercenary marriage that Harry had escaped and the rejoicings that follow his reprieve stress the immensity of the gap which divides these novels from Georgian fiction. While the *mariage de convenance* was accepted as natural in the novel of the '20's and '30's, by the end of the mid-Victorian period it was being condemned on all sides. As more demands were made of, and for, women, and their self-respect increased, they became less inclined to condone the practice of having a mercenary value set upon them. And, on the other hand, among men, as the great tide of sturdy independence and middle-class morality swept the Victorian scene, the fortune hunter was frowned upon, as he pursued his own policy of self-help. This was not to say that the average man did not appreciate his good fortune if he happened to acquire a wife with a certain income of her own. 'Doan't thee marry for munny but goa where munny is', the frequently repeated motto of *The Eustace Diamonds*, was certainly not without some contemporary appeal. But although bartering for marriage settlements was still the fashion in society,* the novelists of the great middle class were opposed to the practice and their heroine was now being sought in marriage for qualities no less sterling than her former dowry. There is a plethora of scathing references to the *mariage de convenance* in mid-Victorian fiction. The whole of *The Newcomes* is a denunciation of the practice; Mr. Dombey's

---

* In *Piccadilly* (1866) which the author, Laurence Oliphant, describes as a 'Fragment of Contemporary Biography' there is considerable, cold-blooded mercantile haggling, in the *haut monde*, over the heroine's matrimonial prospects.

second marriage is a disastrous object lesson; Trollope, too, constantly and sturdily, sets his face against the practice. In *The Small House at Allington*, Crosbie is spared no misery after he has married Lady Alexandrina de Courcy for her money. His repentance begins with his reflections in the railway carriage as they set off on their honeymoon.

'Had he not made a terrible mistake? Of what use to him in life would be that thing of a woman that sat opposite to him? In truth a great punishment had come upon him. He would have been happy with Lily Dale and therefore we may surmise that his unhappiness with Lady Alexandrina would be the greater. There are men who, in marrying such as Lady Alexandrina, would get the article best suited to them; it was in this that Crosbie's failure had been so grievous that he had seen and approved the better course but had chosen for himself to walk in that which was worse.'[18]

Lady Alexandrina would have been the 'article best suited' to many a novel-hero forty years earlier, if only by virtue of her price-tag. And yet she is of no value compared with that set upon Lily Dale, the penniless and proud, not only by readers but, what is more significant, by herself. Lily Dale does not in any way prove herself to be a New Woman in continuing to love the man who jilted her—Anne Elliot had claimed the same privilege for the whole of her sex fifty years earlier, that of 'loving longest when existence or when hope is gone'—but she is sufficiently advanced in independence to prefer a life of celibacy to a second-best marriage. It is true that she does not reject Johnny Eames for the feminist reason that he could not offer her 'equality, community of interest, likeness of intellect', but because of the feminine one, that though he offered her a comfortable home and a wealth of love, she could not look up to him as she would wish to do to her husband. Nevertheless, a charming, desirable, spinster heroine was a new feature for the novel that had not before had any experience of an old maid under forty. And it was some indication that celibacy, under feminist auspices, was not now presenting quite such a grim visage, even to a die-hard like Trollope, when he could contemplate abandoning his heroine to a solitary life and allow her to slight the security that marriage offered—security that had so long been the whole aim

8

of Victorian women—by brushing it aside as a secondary consideration.

There was, however, no doubt at all in Trollope's mind that by rejecting marriage Lily had given up her chance of attaining the fullest and happiest life possible for women. Lily Dale is often put forward as Trollope's favourite heroine, but his admiration for her was tempered by irritation. 'In the love with which Lily Dale has been greeted I have hardly joined with much enthusiasm, feeling that she is somewhat of a French prig . . . It was because Lily could not get over her troubles that people loved her.'

It would have been inconceivable some years earlier that the life of virginity that Lily was philosophically contemplating should have appeared to readers in any other light than that of blighted spinsterhood. To many, judging by the letters of protest Trollope received, it still did. But, by the '60's, feminist propaganda had had a certain effect on society; 'old maids' were being resolutely crowded from the foreground by 'unmarried women'. A life of independence was being decked out in its most cheerful colours, while marriage, with all the talk of its disadvantages and legal snares, took on a somewhat sepia hue. It would have been a hard task to find a Victorian woman who would not have gladly taken the risk of unhappiness in marriage. But the fact that there was such a risk, that the balance was not quite so surely weighted as had till then been assumed with marriage and bliss on one scale and spinsterhood and misery on the other—was a new line of thought that many were following to its logical conclusion.

3. HONOURABLE SPINSTERHOOD

By this time, celibacy, like almost every other matter affecting women, had been to some extent taken under public protection and old maids, from being, in turn, slighted, ignored and deplored, were now in a fair way to being organised. Their problem provoked, between 1860 and 1870, considerable discussion and a number of articles with such unanswerable titles as 'Why are Women Redundant?' or 'What Shall We Do with Our Old Maids?' appeared. There were two main viewpoints; the popular one, upheld by writers like W. R. Greg, was that marriage was the despotic law of life, and that therefore the aim of 'many female reformers and one man of real pre-eminence' to make single life attractive and pleasant for women was misguided and perverted. The better solution was for women to make married life attractive and pleasant for men, so that they would prefer having a wife to keeping a mistress, or, if all else failed, for women to emigrate with a view to marriage across the ocean. The emigration solution, which was constantly being put forward, was considered by the feminists to be no solution at all. Their attitude was that, as thirty per cent. of women in England were unmarried, it would be better to accept the situation and to educate them to support themselves in comfort rather than to ship them off to the colonies like superfluous cattle. The degrading necessity for marriage would no longer exist were women educated for a profession; there would be fewer unions of interest and more of love; and with honourable spinsterhood in the fashion, prostitution would decline and more men would be forced to contemplate marriage.

Such, then, were the two viewpoints. Honourable spinsterhood was as yet only a feminist dream, but public opinion was moving inch by inch in that direction. A more tolerant attitude to old maids was everywhere discernible. They had ceased to be figures of fun, but the prevailing tendency was now to weight them down with their duties to mankind and to deny them the luxury of an individual existence. The figure of Miss Mann or Miss Ainley in *Shirley* (1849) is very different from the former comic spinster, with her lapdog and parrot, as described by Susan Ferrier, but hers is still not an enviable lot, passing her days in her cottage—'a still, dim little place, without a bright hope or near friend in the world.' Caroline Helstone, herself facing, as she thinks, the prospect of spinsterhood, devotes much serious thought to the subject of the rights of the single woman. Under her smooth brown ringlets her brain works busily and she is made the unlikely mouthpiece of many really advanced opinions:

'Where is my place in the world? . . . Ah! I see that is the question which most old maids are puzzled to solve; other people solve it for them by saying, "Your place is to do good to others, to be helpful

whenever help is wanted". That is right in some measure, and a ver
convenient doctrine for the people who hold it; but I perceive tha
certain sets of human beings are very apt to maintain that other set
should give up their lives to them and their service, and then the
requite them by praise; they call them devoted and virtuous. Is thi
enough? Is it to live? Is there not a terrible hollowness, mockery
want, craving in that existence which is given away to others, fo
want of something of your own to bestow it on? I suspect there is
Does virtue lie in abnegation of self? I do not believe it. Undu
humility makes tyranny; weak concession creates selfishness . . .
believe single women should have more to do—better chances o
interesting and profitable occupation than they possess now. Peopl
hate to be reminded of ills they are unwilling or unable to remed
. . . Old maids, like the houseless and unemployed poor, should no
ask for a place and an occupation in the world, the demand disturb
the happy and rich; it disturbs parents.'

'At What Age Are Ladies Considered Old Maids?' asks Eudor;
anxiously in the correspondence columns of the *Englishwomen'*
Domestic Magazine of 1860, and receives the reassuring reply:

Single ladies are old maids at thirty if their hearts do not beat wit
sympathetic emotion at the joy of youth or the sorrows of age. The
are not old maids at fifty if they can look kindly on all the world, tal
cheerfully on all womanly topics and eschew scandal and eccentricity
We know four 'unmarried ladies' whose ages range from 40-60, wh
are soft-hearted, generous, industrious, pious and happy sisters, livin;
together (a life of celibacy through accident—not choice) and thei
friends speak of them as 'unmarried' not 'old maids'.

Such generous tolerance of their celibacy (if 'through acciden
—not choice') was all very well and old maids appreciated th
fact that the conditions of their lives were becoming less and les
severe. But some were a little alarmed to find that their responsi
bilities were increasing in the same ratio. In the *North Britisl*
Review of 1862 there is an illuminating article, 'My Life an(
What Shall I do With It?' by 'An Old Maid'. The writer point
out that spinsters have gained much socially and æsthetically
by having passed from the 'withered prude' of earlier fiction t(
the serene, consoling spinster of contemporary fiction, but goe
on to confess that 'Good books can sometimes awaken very
wicked thoughts'. It is not a new sphere of action that singl(
women need but more perfect freedom and expansion in thei

own, with power to develop their organising ability, to indulge
in 'housekeeping on a larger scale', in charitable, penal and
reformatory institutions, to devote themselves to constructive
social work—anything, in short, that will prevent them from
submerging themselves and their personalities completely in
other people's lives and interests, with no return for their sacri-
fices.

The 'unmarried woman', then, was awakening to a consciousness of her duty not only to the world, but to herself. The new
attitude was that the more responsibilities she undertook, the
more penal and reformatory institutions she continued to run,
the higher her status would become.

It is quite striking to observe how much the useful power and
influence of women has developed of late years. Unattached ladies,
such as widows and unmarried women have quite ample work to do
in the world for the good of others to absorb all their powers . . . I
was much struck by the remark made by Mr. Deshmukh, a very
superior young Hindu. He said that it was most important for society
to have some unmarried women to give a tone to it. You know, they
have none in India.[19]

The majority of novelists, however, had not attained to Mr.
Deshmukh's superior degree of enlightenment. The spinster of
fiction, though philanthropically minded, was still in the main
considered, as Mrs. Linton impressively put it, 'as a violation of
a natural law and the confessed inability of man to render
nature and society harmonious'. The old maid had now to endure
pitying headshakes rather than contemptuous smiles. In *Sowing
the Wind* (1867) Mrs. Linton painted a pathetic picture.

Poor Rosa Varley! . . . There are many Rosas in our country
places, the potentialities of faithful wives and tender mothers withering away within the dry hush of loneliness . . . virgins not quite of
the sun but of the dead cold moon, withering and wasting as the
years roll on. Their fate is a sad one . . . among the saddest of all.

To a married woman their fate no doubt did seem irretrievably
desolate. And to a married man, like Trollope, even more so.
Considering them wasted women, he never had much time to
spare for them in his novels. Aspasia Fitzgibbon he summed up
in six words—'Old Maid, over forty, very plain'—and even when

he did devote a little more space to spinsterhood he gave an impression of ineffable dreariness. Miss MacNulty, the indigent
spinster of *The Eustace Diamonds*, for instance, was

> . . . as utterly destitute of possessions or means of existence as any
> unfortunate, well-born and moderately well-educated middle-aged
> woman in London. To live upon her friends, such as they might be,
> was the only mode of life within her reach. It was not that she had
> chosen such dependence; nor indeed had she endeavoured to reject
> it. It had come to her as a matter of course. Either that or the poor
> house. As to earning her bread except by the attendance which a
> poor friend gives—the idea of any possibility that way had never
> entered her head. She could do nothing except dress like a lady, with
> the smallest possible cost, and endeavour to be obliging.[20]

Trollope saw no redeeming feature in celibacy and said so
bluntly. Some writers there were, however, who determinedly
looked on the bright side. In *Passages in the Life of an Old Maid*,
the anon. author, I. C. K., provided a spinster who was neither
frustrated nor discontented with her lot but indulged her wit
at the expense of the other sex. Referring to the cliché, 'old
maids leading apes in hell', she observed archly:

> What particular sin old maids have committed that they should be
> condemned to lead about apes hereafter in that place which is never
> mentioned to ears polite I am at a loss to conceive . . . My solution
> is that descendants of Mother Eve must suffer punishment for her sin
> some time or other, and that if old maids are not condemned to lead
> apes and fools in this world like many married women their punish-
> ment must come sooner or later and therefore, though they escape it,
> it will follow them in the next world.[21]

With a somewhat less heavy hand, Trollope dealt with the
fashionable topic of a large, middle-class, female emigration in
Phineas Finn. Lady Baldock's present hobby—a Female Protes-
tant Unmarried Women's Emigration Society—was the subject
of discussion:

> 'But it is a perilous affair for me,' said Violet, 'as my aunt wishes
> me to go out as a sort of leading Protestant unmarried female emi-
> grant pioneer myself.'
> 'You don't mean that,' said Lord Fawn with much anxiety.
> 'Of course you'll go,' said Phineas. 'I should if I were you.'
> 'I am in doubt,' said Violet.

'It is such a grand prospect,' said he, 'such an opening in life. So much excitement, you know: and such a useful career.'[22]

The novelist was obviously not yet disposed to take the 'unmarried woman' as seriously as she took herself. Despite its grand prospects, celibacy was still far from rivalling marriage as a career for an enterprising young woman—and even the most advanced and emancipated writers stopped short of a perennial spinster ideal of womanhood.* And although the novelists' ideal heroine had been played upon by so many external influences of late that they were often unsure just what she was really like, of one thing they were still certain: her ultimate fate must be marriage.

But, at the same time, they were keenly and uncomfortably aware that marriage was not what it used to be before John Stuart Mill turned his coldly analytical brain upon it. Since the feminists had raised the hare of 'equality, community of interests and likeness of intellect', they had had to become more specific about the inducements that matrimony held out for the heroine of 1873. Any sort of marriage would not now satisfy the reading public as the happy ending to a novel; new and exacting standards had been set. And although there was still enough gilt left on the magic phrase 'an offer' to allure Victorians, they were less dazzled by its splendour, and even at times found themselves casting a critical and apprehensive eye upon the gingerbread realities of the marriage state.

* By the time, however, that Gissing wrote *The Odd Women* (1893) the intelligent, charming, unmarried woman had come to have definite possibilities for the novelist that the old maid stock character never possessed.

CHAPTER V

The Social Evil

1. A WALL OF ADAMANT

It is as well that other sources of information exist as to the conduct and moral standards of Victorians between the years 1837 and 1853 than the novels published at that time. For the existence of immorality was not denied by Victorians—it was merely ignored—and although, here and there, we find a writer intrepid enough to lift a corner of the veil of secrecy that shrouded the *demi-monde*, no one was prepared to jeopardise his sales by tearing it down completely. It is typical of this evasive era that we may learn more of the actual state of affairs from prefaces than from the novels themselves.

A preface by Dickens in 1841, for instance, gives an oblique indication of the prevailing moral attitude. Although nothing could have been more painfully discreet than his treatment of Nancy in *Oliver Twist*—the unworldly might still have been in doubt as to her profession when they reached the last page—the wrath of the sanctimonious descended upon him. And, riled by such unlooked-for criticism, 'on some high moral grounds in some high moral quarters', he gave them, in his preface to the third edition, something more to think about by referring to her roundly as a prostitute and defending his motives with spirit. He insisted that he had endeavoured

'. . . no less consulting my own taste, than the manners of the age, while I painted it (Vice) in all its fallen and degraded aspect, to banish from the lips of the lowest character I introduced, any expression that could by possibility offend; and rather to lead to the unavoidable inference that its existence was of the most debased and vicious kind than to prove it elaborately by words and deeds. In the case of the girl, in particular, I kept this intention constantly in view.'

And, indeed, Dickens had some right to feel injured. For the benefit of his public he had divined springs of sentiment in the hardened sinner which had gushed up in such spontaneous tributes as: ' "Oh, lady, lady!" she said, clasping her hands passionately before her face, "if there was more like you there would be fewer like me—there would—there would!" '

In his own practical experience with prostitutes, he was scarcely paid such dividends in gratitude. Amid the multitudes of small channels for aiding the poor that coursed through the '30's and '40's it was inevitable that there should be several tributaries for the purpose of reclaiming Magdalens. By 1860 there were more than forty refuges and reformatories established for young women 'desirous of returning to the paths of virtue',[1] via a course of washing, needlework and much wholesome discipline. Not perhaps surprisingly, there was no eager waiting list of applicants for entry to such institutions, and in 1846, Dickens, with a 3,000-word epistle, started off a lengthy correspondence with the Baroness Burdett-Coutts in support of her plan to found a Home which might, above all, 'Tempt Women to Virtue'. There were already some such schemes on similar lines afoot in London, from which they proposed to learn; but, with Dickens' imaginative enthusiasm and the Baroness Coutts' capital, Urania Cottage, Shepherd's Bush, appeared to stand a good chance of becoming a favourite postal address of penitents. It was Dickens' aim to make the harsh clang, as the gates of respectability swung to behind her, fall more sweetly on the prostitute's ear. He was fertile in proposals for distinguishing the more promising among them from the others; for doing away with the monotony and 'the almost insupportable extent to which other asylums carried the words and forms of religion'; for adding excitement with a competitive Mark System and optimism with a reiteration of the likelihood of a Return to Happiness. For although he 'did not propose to put the possibility of marriage before them as the immediate end and object to be gained—assuredly to keep it in view as the possible consequence of a sincere, true, practical repentance and an altered life.'[2]

His approach to the question was a characteristic blend of dramatic pathos and common sense. The letter that he designed should be slipped into the hand of every penitent as she entered the home was a masterly piece of sentiment which would have touched later, more appreciative, audiences to tears : 'If ever you have wished (I know you must have done so sometimes) for a chance of rising out of your sad life—having friends, a quiet home, means of being useful to yourself and others, peace of mind, self-respect, everything you have lost, pray read it attentively—reflect upon it afterwards.'

On the other hand, his reception of the pattern of drab, cotton material called 'Derry', that Baroness Burdett-Coutts sent to him as suitable for overalls for the inmates, was marked by shrewd insight.

'I return Derry. I have no doubt that it's a capital article, but it's a mortal dark colour. Colour these people always want and colour (as altered to fancy) I would always give them. In these cast-iron and mechanical days I think even such a garnish to the dish of their monotonous and hard lives of unspeakable importance. Who is Derry that he should make quakers of us all whether we will or no !'

But even with Dickens' sturdy ebullience and sympathy, his untiring labour, his mark system, the Refuge, after over ten discouraging years in which failures far outnumbered success, had to be given up. His dealings with prostitutes, however, did not affect his treatment of them in his novels; his reading-public would not have relished frankness. A great lady like the Baroness Burdett-Coutts might, with impunity, interest herself in the fate of outcasts, but the normal, middle-class, philanthropic sphere of the '40's did not extend so far. Under the amorphous term 'fallen women', the Victorian housewife mentally slumped together girls driven through want to prostitution, *filles-de-joie*, working women who had met with a 'misfortune', innocent girls who had been seduced or tricked by a false marriage. William Bell Scott complained of women that

They shut their eyes to every form of the Social Evil and take it as an impertinence in any man, poet especially, who draws their attention to these matters; and I have never known the woman yet, however 'strongminded', who will allow any poem to lie on her table or within sight that has any allusion to Cyprians or bastards. 'Serve them right' is the verdict of the sweetest and gentlest of creatures.[3]

But while certain men took pride in feeling compassion for Magdalens, and blamed women of their own class for their hardness of heart, they neglected to acknowledge any responsibility themselves for the prostitute's existence. In all his interchange of letters about the 'battered and tarnished images of God', Dickens never once makes reference to masculine culpability; the battering and tarnishing might have been accomplished by remote, inhuman agencies, for any indication he gives of the process leading to the *fait accompli*. In *David Copperfield* (1849), the character of Martha is obscured by conventional darkness and gloom. She makes her few brief appearances only at night, slipping out of the shadows for a few moments to disappear again into them, as wretched a figure as ever. Dickens' description of her, hovering on the brink of the 'dreadful river', is well in the tradition of damp, dark destitution already established by one or two poets, like Bell Scott and Hood. *Rosabell*, written in 1837 by Bell Scott after an encounter* with a prostitute and published some years later, was presumably one of those poems about the Social Evil which were debarred from Victorian tables, although it was innocent of both Cyprians and bastards. It was, on the contrary, the story of a sempstress, led astray by the bad company of the other girls in the workroom. From neglect, at first, of her mother's advice.

> . . . . to rise betimes,
> To dress quite plain, to lace her boots
> As she had always done . . .

she went from bad to worse. Bell Scott, in tracing her downward path, asked, with stern, Scottish pity, the question that so touched Rossetti's heart:

> Can the outcast retrace her steps?
> Would any mourn with her although
> She watered the earth with tears? . . .

* Bell Scott, looking back on the incident later, remarked: 'To me this sentiment (of purity) was a wall of adamant, invisible but of absolute power of moral defence. I say this that there may be no question about my relation to a girl I met on the street one night . . .' From behind his wall of adamant, Bell Scott attempted to evangelise Rosabell, but, discouraged by her fatalistic attitude, had to be content with going home and making a 'history for her as one of the doomed' —the manuscript of which he carefully carried in his portmanteau to London.

And hearts as innocent as hers,
As blindly shall succeed, shall take
Leap after leap into the dark,
Blaspheming soul and sense at once
And every lamp on every street
Shall light their wet feet down to death . . .

In *The Bridge of Sighs* (1846), Hood, with some skill, evades naming the profession of his One More Unfortunate, Weary of Breath—although a slanting rebuke to Dissolute Man leaves it in little doubt. Pity is once again the predominant note. Pity from a standpoint of virtuous detachment. As a test piece for Victorian lungs and hearts, the poem soon attained deserved popularity for after-dinner elocution.

Take her up tenderly
Lift her with care,
Fashioned so slenderly
Young and so fair . . .

Dickens' treatment of Martha, then, was stereotyped enough. Except perhaps in one particular. Unlike her predecessors, she was not forced to seek her redemption in death. Her sin, it is true, was spoken of in guarded whispers. 'A poor wurem as is trod under foot by all the town' was Ham's description of her. But Dickens remained faithful to his principles of ultimate marriage for a sincere penitent and married her off, in the far-distant Bush, to a man who could not afford to pick and choose as 'wives are very sceerce there'. The penitents from Urania Cottage, on the other hand, had had a different destination. After their probation period they had been despatched—with Dickens' nice sense of the fitness of things—to the Cape of Good Hope.

On the whole, however, it is the melodramatic rather than the practical that characterised Dickens' approach to the loss of reputation in women. The seduction of little Em'ly is lapped by romantic pathos from start to finish, from her tearful farewell letter, with its terrible proviso 'If he don't bring me back a lady . . .' to Mr. Peggoty's touching picture of her, sorrowing away her days. Also in the Bush. After Steerforth has appeased justice with his life, there are no more recriminations. Dickens, having shaken a reproachful head, felt he had gone far enough and declined to draw any general social implications.

What of the other early Victorian novelists? Thackeray, who was more adept than any other writer of his time at stirring forbidden waters without getting himself splashed, ventured towards the topic of morality with a careful recklessness that quite deceived his most ardent admirer, Miss Charlotte Brontë. Seldom has anything penned in frank esteem sounded more like satire, to a later generation, than her misguided preface to the second edition of *Jane Eyre*, which she dedicated to W. M. Thackeray, 'the tribute of a total stranger'.

I would remind [the timorous or carping few] . . . of certain simple truths.

Conventionality is not morality; self-righteousness is not religion. . . . These things are diametrically opposed; they are as distinct as is vice from virtue.

There is a man in our own days whose words are not framed to tickle delicate ears. . . . Is the satirist of *Vanity Fair* admired in high places? I cannot tell . . . but I see in him an intellect profounder and more unique than his contemporaries have yet recognised because I regard him as the first social regenerator of the day . . . They say he is like Fielding; they talk of his wit, humour, comic powers. He resembles Fielding as an eagle does a vulture. Fielding could stoop on carrion, but Thackeray never does.

The satirist of *Vanity Fair* was certainly admired in high places—but not for the attributes so enthusiastically ascribed to him by Miss Brontë. Indeed, the famous scenes between the Marquis of Steyne and Becky might appear to have been designed for the especial purpose of 'tickling delicate ears'. There could be, at first, no doubt in readers' minds as to Becky's guilt: 'You innocent! Damn you—— You innocent! Why, every trinket you have on your body is paid for by me. Innocent, by——! You're as innocent as your mother, the ballet girl, and your husband, the bully.'

But this was somewhat too outspoken for Thackeray to be content to leave it at that. A doubt must be raised to satisfy the more prudish among his readers. 'What *had* happened? Was she guilty or not? She said not; but who could tell what was truth which came from those lips, or if that corrupt heart was in this case pure?'

And still not content to leave well alone, Thackeray returns to the topic, a few chapters further on, with a semblance of thwarted frankness.

We must pass over a part of Mrs. Rebecca Crawley's biography with that lightness and delicacy which the world demands—the moral world, that has, perhaps, no particular objection to vice, but an insuperable repugnance to hearing vice called by its proper name . . . and a polite public will no more bear to read an authentic description of vice than a truly refined English or American female will permit the word 'breeches' to be pronounced in her chaste hearing . . . And so when Becky is out of the way, be sure that she is not particularly well employed, and that the less that is said about her doings is, in fact, the better.

It was Thackeray's misfortune that he felt so keenly the magnetic power of moral considerations. For despising, and yet deferring to public opinion, as he did, it was impossible for him to tackle the issues squarely. He had to be content with impatient complaints against the restrictions put upon him by society, with innuendoes and with semi-revelations. In the 1850 preface to *Pendennis*, he states his position:

Even the gentlemen of our age—this is an attempt to describe one of them, no better nor worse than most educated men—even those we cannot show as they are, with the notorious foibles and selfishnesses of their lives and their education. Since the author of Tom Jones was buried, no writer of fiction among us has been permitted to depict, to his utmost power, a man. We must drape him, and give him a certain conventional simper. Society will not tolerate the Natural in our Art. Many ladies have remonstrated and subscribers have left me, because in the course of the story I described a young man resisting and affected by temptation . . . A little more frankness than is customary has been attempted in this story.

The little more frankness did not extend to Pen's sex life, which was discreetly veiled, nor was the fashionable gospel of two standards of morality ever seriously challenged by Thackeray, despite occasional references to the inequality of the burden borne by the sexes:

Alas, the life of such boys does not bear telling altogether. I wish it did. I ask you, does yours? As long as what we call our honour is clear I suppose your mind is pretty easy. Women are pure but not men. Women are unselfish but not men. And I would not wish to say of poor Arthur Pendennis that he was worse than his neighbours, only that his neighbours are bad for the most part.

Many less great than Thackeray, less concerned with important moral problems, have contrived to avoid—as he has not —the stigma of hypocrisy. For, always eager to thrust forward, he was also alertly ready to draw back in time; to savour the thrill of the situation without its danger. In so doing he ran a constant risk of anti-climax. It is certainly not unmixed relief that the reader feels in *Esmond* after his emotions and fears have been titillated about Beatrix's honour, after the Colonel and Frank have ridden post to Castlewood and hammered on the gates to demand entrance, only to find that (in the Prince's words), 'Morbleu! there has been no dishonour—only a little harmless playing', that was meant to end seriously.

Thackeray's somewhat tortuous treatment of morality themes is in marked contrast to that of his exact contemporaries. J. A. Froude's *The Lieutenant's Daughter* (1847) startles, in view of its date, by its frank and sympathetic treatment of its prostitute heroine. The story, a series of visions reminiscent of *A Christmas Carol* in its time-element juggling, opens with a graveyard scene in which a wretched outcast commits suicide on her parents' grave. Her story is then traced backwards to find where the blame lies for her tragic ending. She is shown to be completely undeserving of her fate—a young orphan without protector or adviser, who has believed the promises of a rich young rake and become enmeshed in the net of procuresses. Froude not only flagellates her seducer; he stresses how important is the part that Chance has played in her downfall by sketching, in an alternative vision, the churchyard scene that would have occurred had Catherine's father lived a few years longer—a happy christening party coming out of the church, with the charming young wife and mother in their midst. 'There but for the grace of God go I'—the sentiment at the core of Froude's story—was not one which would have occurred to many Victorian women in considering the prostitute's lot—and the admirable candour of the dialogue would scarcely have recommended the book for female reading. This quality is especially marked when the procuresses are chatting together about the tricks of their trade and when the reporters are writing up an account of the girl's suicide, which will not offend the gentry:

'What d'ye say to something touching and romantic? . . . No, hang it, that won't do either; we mustn't make it interesting. Vice and suicide. Aye, that's right. Vice and suicide. This morning an inquest was held at the Royal Arms, Exmouth, on the body of a young woman——'
'Female, Ned, female; woman don't sound respectable.'
'Well, on the body of a young female, who was recognised by several of the inhabitants as Catherine Gray, and from her appearance must have been lately given to abandoned habits. (That's moral, eh, Jack?) She left Exmouth, it will be remembered, a year since with a gentleman (whose name out of deference to his honoured and respected relatives, we think it best to conceal), under circumstances betraying peculiar ingratitude; and it was for some time a subject of great alarm to the friends of the gentleman, that she might have been privately married to him. From this fear, however, they were happily soon relieved, as he was recovered from his abandoned companion, and she had not since been heard of. A person answering the description of deceased had been seen the day before in the neighbourhood in a state of extreme destitution, and this morning she was found in the churchyard quite dead.'[4]

Less outspoken, but still, in its entirety, an early condemnation of profligacy, *Wildfell Hall* (1848) exposes the sorrows of life with a fashionable, drunken young reprobate. The heroine, Helen, although a long-suffering young woman, has the Brontë characteristic of heavy-handed tactlessness. Conceiving it her duty to remain with her husband as long as humanly possible (until her four-year-old, Arthur, begins to tipple and swear like papa), she never loses an opportunity of pointing out his delinquencies to him. Huntingdon's deathbed, as protracted for this Lovelace as Clarissa's, while unquestionably an awful object lesson, must have, in some unregenerate breasts, kindled a flicker of sympathy for the sinner:

'You know,' said I, a little surprised at his manner, 'that I am willing to do anything I can to relieve you.'
'Yes, now, my immaculate angel; but when once you have secured your reward, and find yourself in heaven, and me howling in hellfire, catch you lifting a finger to serve me then! No, you'll look com-

placently on, and not so much as dip the tip of your finger in water to cool my tongue!'

'If so, it will be because of the great gulf over which I cannot pass; and if I could look complacently in such a case it would only be from the assurance that you were being purified from your sins and fitted to enjoy the happiness I felt. But are you determined, Arthur, that I shall not meet you in heaven?'

'Humph! What should I do there, I should like to know?'

'Indeed I cannot tell; and I fear it is too certain that your tastes and feelings must be widely altered before you can have any enjoyment there.'

In the same year, in *Mary Barton*, Mrs. Gaskell contrived to dispel a little of the darkness that had gathered around unfortunate women by her sympathetic study of the prostitute, Esther.

He turned and saw that the woman who stood by him was of no doubtful profession. It was told by her faded finery, all unfit to meet the pelting of that pitiless storm; he saw at once the long-lost Esther; she who had caused his wife's death. Much was like the gay creature of former years; but the glaring paint, the sharp features, the changed expression of the whole . . .

It is in this novel that there is some attempt to probe into the mind of a woman who has lost her reputation, to convey her desperate impotence rather than her degradation. 'To whom shall the outcast prostitute tell her tale? Who will give her help in the day of need? Hers is the leper-sin and all stand aloof dreading to be counted unclean . . .'

The reason for Esther's downfall was the usual one of passion and betrayed love. In *Alton Locke* (1850) Kingsley did not scruple to replace the more romantic motive by one of practical economics and gave a realistic picture of poverty-stricken, diseased households in which seamstresses were driven to the streets by starvation. The only 'honest woman' of one such establishment is a sick girl who rejoices in her disfigurement by small-pox and consequent exemption from prostitution. Into her lips he puts an impassioned plea:

'Tell them it'll never prosper. I know it is want that drives them to t as it drives all of us—but tell them it's best to starve and die honest girls than to go about with the shame and the curse of God on their hearts for the sake of keeping this poor miserable vile body together a few short years more in this world o' sorrow.'

Lizzy had had her face on her hands the greater part of this speech. Now she looked up passionately, almost fiercely. 'Repent— I have repented—I repent of it every hour—I hate myself—hate all the world because of it; but I must—I must. I cannot see her starve and I cannot starve myself.'

It is to women that Kingsley makes his appeal—an appeal from those in the depths to 'real ladies' on the heights. There is as yet no mention made of the part that could be played by men, by 'real gentlemen', in the reclamation scheme: 'O Woman! Woman! only true missionary of civilisation and brotherhood and gentle forgiving charity, it is in thy power and perhaps in thine only, to bind up the broken-hearted, to preach deliverance to the captives. One real lady who should dare to stoop, what might she not do with us—with our sisters.'

The ugly little episode in *Pendennis*, in which Laura and Helen encounter Fanny Bolton in Pen's sick-room, gives a glimpse of two good women in action against a supposed transgressor. Without hesitation, they leap to the wrong conclusion about her relations with Pen, and with remorseless cruelty show her the door. While Thackeray felt rueful misgiving at the primitive emotions of jealousy, predatory affection and suspicion underlying the behaviour of virtuous women, he acquiesced in their necessity. The purity of women was one of the safeguards of society; 'gentle forgiving charity' was sufficiently exacted by masculine shortcomings, without women extending their tolerance to their own sex.

With *Alton Locke* and *Pendennis* we find ourselves on the threshold of the period of mid-Victorianism in England. With the conflicts and nervous uneasiness of the '40's safely behind it, the nation was eager to settle down to an era in which everything was weatherproof, stout-principled and prosperous, in which everything, as they themselves would have put it, was according to Cocker. The policy of secrecy and hypocritical silence, observed in the early years of the Victorian age towards moral matters, had been largely predetermined by the influences of the Evangelicals and of the Regency court. Prudery and puritanism, concomitants of the movement of religious regeneration at the end of the eighteenth century, had steadily gained ground in certain sections of the community and had been strengthened by the resentment felt by the middle classes at the frivolity and unblushing dissipation of court circles. In the '30's the Evangelical movement reached its peak and the upper classes also found themselves catered for by the religious enthusiasm of the Oxford Movement. So that when the Victorian age opened with the middle classes, politically, in the ascendancy, the entire nation was disposed to take its soul more seriously than it had for years, to follow solidly the Sabbath ideal of virtue, the weekday one of respectability.

Now, however, in the '50's, a new influence was making itself felt. The Saints of Clapham and the sinners of Brighton seemed like insubstantial shadows of a past age, in comparison with the ideal family at Osborne. The direct lead had been given from the throne. Not only towards a virtuous family life but towards —which was even more important in its effect upon Victorian moral attitudes—the sanctification of its privacy. Reluctant to share with anyone the delights of domesticity, of Albert as husband and father, of Pussy and Bertie and their droll little ways, Victoria withdrew first to Osborne; then to the Scottish baronial seclusion of Balmoral. There, at last, they were safe from intrusion. After its first surprise, the nation looked on sympathetically and the Englishman's home straightway became his castle also. The Stuart tartan rugs and deerheads might be lacking but the ménage was characterised by the same disinterest in the affairs of others, the same inbred contentment, that gave to their outlook that element of unimaginative complacency which, infused into mid-Victorian morality, produced its distinctive blend.

The more insulated their homes became from outside contacts, the more exaggerated the evils and dangers of the world appeared to women, and the more urgent the necessity for men to keep all such knowledge from them. In the evening round the fire, while vice prowled outside in the dark streets, it was only from books supplied by dependable lending libraries that the head of the family chose to read aloud to his brood. And consequently, in the month of March, 1853, many a firm, sonorous Victorian voice must, in the course of the evening's reading, suddenly have faltered, in outraged surprise—and then died away altogether, as the covers of the latest book from Mudie's were hastily clapped together. For that Select Library, which had the largest circulation of any, had, with strange disregard of possible perversion of morals, neglected to exclude Mrs. Gaskell's new novel *Ruth* from its list.

2. INNOCENCE AND IGNORANCE

The storm of protests, reviews and discussion which followed the publication of *Ruth* give a revealing picture of the ethical background of England at this time. The simplicity of the theme of the novel was more than compensated for by the complexity of the emotions it aroused. Ruth, a beautiful innocent girl, abandoned by her lover before the birth of her child, is befriended by a Non-conformist minister and his sister who pass her off to their congregation as a widow. Although Ruth is unmercifully boycotted once her secret is discovered, she finds her salvation in her love for her child and in the sick-nursing which leads to her death. Such was the story which was withdrawn from at least one circulating library as 'unfit for family reading'.

What, then, was there new in *Ruth*? . . . The especial significance of the novel lay in the fact that the unmarried mother, who had lurked in the background of so many novels, was not only brought into the light of day but—what shocked the susceptibilities of the reading-public even more—was attired in robes till then sacred to the virgin heroine. *Ruth* was not a novel in which consideration of moral standards was relegated to a few minor episodes which could be skimmed over surreptitiously. The ideas were set forth with such candour that to many they appeared as revolutionary doctrines; the question of the comparative importance of sins, for instance, was raised by Mrs. Gaskell, who made no secret of her belief that an inadvertent moral lapse was less culpable than ingrained, fanatical intolerance.

'If there be one sin I hate, I utterly loathe more than all others, it is wantonness. It includes all other sins! . . .'
'I was so young! . . .'
'The more depraved, the more disgusting, you.'

Again, Mrs. Gaskell departed from the usual idea of the child of sin as a 'badge of shame', and put into Mr. Benson's lips an avowal of the purifying influence of the child upon the future life of an unmarried mother.

'The sin appears to me to be quite distinct from its consequences. In the eye of God she is exactly the same as if the life she had led has left no trace behind. If her life has hitherto been self-seeking and wickedly thoughtless here is the very instrument to make her forget herself and be thoughtful for another. Teach her to reverence her child and this reverence will shut out sin; it will be purification.'

Moreover, there was no attempt to slur over the guilt of the dissolute lover; the tolerant 'wild oats' attitude had no appeal for Mrs. Gaskell. 'Men may call such actions as yours youthful follies. There is another name for them with God'!

And finally, in drawing two such figures as Mr. and Miss Benson, beset by worldly misgivings but generous and sturdily broad-minded, Mrs. Gaskell placed before her readers an example of Christian charity which she apparently thought not beyond their powers to emulate.

She over-estimated their capabilities. Although she admitted that she knew before what might be the result of writing on such a subject, the violence of the abuse hurled at her took her unawares. Indignant letters, shocked protests, insulting or pained reviews poured in and she confessed to having 'taken leave of my "respectable" friends up and down the country'. A friend, outside that category, commented:

Lily herself has been rather ailing and low-spirited lately; she takes to heart very much all the evil that is said of *Ruth* and, of course, a great deal *is* said; among others at Knutsford . . . But old Lady Stanley sends word, with some truth, "that all the men who are worth caring about like it; it is only the poor ignorant women who are shocked"; and Bishop Stanley's widow writes that her sons and all the younger men she hears speak of it say that "it is one of the most virtue-stirring works they have ever read".[5]

Bishop Stanley's widow's sons, however, were unhappily in a minority. Celibate Oxford read and condemned the book. Josephine Butler sat silent and dissenting among her husband's colleagues at social gatherings, listening to

expressions of judgement which seemed to me false—fatally false. A moral lapse in a woman was spoken of as an immeasurably worse

thing than in a man, there was no comparison to be formed between
them. A pure woman, it was reiterated, should be absolutely ignorant
of a certain class of evils in the world, albeit those evils bore with a
murderous cruelty on other women. One young man solemnly declared that he would not allow his own mother to read such a book
as that under discussion.[6]

The young man's filial solicitude was to go for nought. Ten
years later it was difficult for any mother to keep her innocence
in the face of the revelations brought to the surface by Mrs.
Butler's moral campaign. And it was, as Mrs. Butler later remarked, such observations as his, that confirmed her in her
opinions, which were already in revolt against certain theories of
society and induced her to begin her work in Oxford on behalf
of destitute women.

The critics of *Ruth* soon divided themselves into three groups.
Those—the majority—who condemned the book outright and
thought it should never have been written; those—like Dickens
and Kingsley,* John Forster and Mrs. Jameson—who considered
it a timely and courageous protest against 'the demoralising
laxity of principle'[7] of the day; and those—the few—who
believed that Mrs. Gaskell had not gone far enough. Charlotte
Brontë, for instance, objected to the death of Ruth which she
felt unnecessary after protracted atonement, and, while praising
the general outline of the story in a letter to Mrs. Gaskell, asked
'Why must we shut the book weeping?' W. R. Greg, in an article
on 'The False Morality of Lady Novelists'[8] went much further
and accused the authoress of exaggerating the importance of
Ruth's sin which arose merely from ignorance. Any moral lapse
(using 'moral' in its usual sexual implication) was, in his opinion,
much less culpable than greed, malignity, hypocrisy or many
another vice, and the real sinner of the novel was, not Ruth,
but the pharisaical parishioner, Bradshaw, who was first to condemn her.

An article in the *Westminster Review* entitled *Ruth* and
Villette (written by G. H. Lewes) expressed similar views. It

---

* Kingsley, for example, wrote to Mrs. Gaskell: 'Among all my large
acquaintance I never heard but one unanimous opinion of the beauty
and righteousness of the book and that, above all, from real ladies and
really good women.'

pointed out that Ruth was seduced under such extenuating circumstances that the question of guilt was reduced to a point of casuistry and that, although Ruth might have much to regret, she could scarcely, in her conscience, have much to repent. 'We confess that for the sake of the teaching we should have preferred Ruth to be more homely and less richly endowed in good qualities and looks. We should have preferred a more simple trust in the principles involved and less attempt to interest and propitiate the reader by all manner of graceful accessories'.

The asphodel beauty of Ruth, however, may well have drawn many nearer than ever before to the edge of that uninviting bog of moral considerations, which they had skirted till then.

Ruth is the story of a seduction—a subject of a most delicate nature which has rarely, if ever, been looked fairly in the face and one which, of all others, it is the rarest to hear a rational word spoken about. The circulating libraries have provided an abundance of sickly sentimentality, with heroines striving to atone by consumption or a broken heart for a lapse of virtue—or frigid barren morality, under which a luckless maiden lingers through the remainder of her days under a deadly weight of patronage and encouragement. The authoress of *Ruth* approaches the subject like a woman, and a truly delicate-minded woman.

Ruth was not the only artistic achievement upon a moral theme in the early '50's. About the same time as it was published, no less than three painters were working along similar lines; Millais on 'Virtue and Vice', Holman Hunt on 'The Awakened Conscience' and Rossetti on 'Found'. The latter's idea was taken from Bell Scott's *Rosabell*—the title of which was later changed to *Mary Anne* to please Rossetti—and showed the encounter between the lost girl and her former rustic lover, Andrew, who has come to town to sell his calf. This subject, which Ruskin thought a 'dreadfully difficult one', Rossetti took very seriously indeed; he first found a calf and then spent a winter painting it. There are frequent solicitous references to 'Gabriel's calf' in pre-Raphaelite diaries of that winter. Unfortunately for Madox Brown his house was nearest to the farm which owned the calf and Rossetti came to stay, dressed in Madox Brown's 'great-coat and breeches (which I want)' and disposing of an unlimited supply of food and turpentine. Even to facilitate the production of a moral masterpiece, however, his host could stand only so much, and the entry in his diary, for the 16th December, reads:

This morning, 16th: Gabriel not yet having done his cart and talking quite freely about several days yet, having been here since the 1st November and not seeming to notice any hints . . . Emma being within a week of her confinement and he having his bed on the floor of the parlour one week now and not getting up till 11 . . . besides my finances being reduced to £2 12s. 6d, which must last until 20th January, I told him delicately he must go, or go home at night by the bus . . .⁹

It was not surprising that Rossetti should have felt enthusiastic about a Magdalen theme nor was it startling—although Rossetti seemed to find it so—that Millais and Hunt should also have begun pictures on a 'modern subject'. 'It would have been impossible,' wrote Ruskin, to the aggrieved Rossetti, 'for men of such eyes and hearts as Millais and Hunt to walk the streets of London or watch the things that pass each day and not to discover also what there was in them to be shown and painted.'¹⁰ But the pre-Raphaelites had not only walked the streets of London. They had patrolled them:

'They instituted search parties for models, turning out in groups of 2's and 3's so as to cover the pavement and not let a likely one slip past them. Rescue of the Fallen' (ante-dating the tactics of Butler and Gladstone) 'they took in their stride, expostulating, pleading. Millais and Deverell were generally spokesmen and led a band each— the two handsomest young fellows in London and (Allingham'd wager) the most innocent, patrolling all the evening, accosting and probably being accosted.'¹¹

In the years that followed it very gradually became possible for others to take an interest in the welfare of outcasts, in the name of Charity, under whose fair, fluttering banner the respectable could march. Women were slowly realising, not only that there were such destitutes in the world, but also that it would not be considered unwomanly were they to admit to such a knowledge. The attitude of the '50's was, however, rather one of moral salvage than of regeneration and reform. A tentative movement was afoot to raise the prostitute from the depths, but the increased tolerance towards women, visible for instance, in

an article by Mrs. Craik in *A Woman's Thoughts about Women*
(1858), was not counterbalanced by new severity towards masculine incontinence. In her view, Eve, 'mercifully constituted with
less temptation to sin than men', must bear the consequence of
her guilt alone, and the remedies suggested are exclusively designed for use 'After the Fall'. She addressed herself to 'the
ordinary middle rank of unmarried female', leaving 'the other
class, who make a trade of sin, to the philanthropist and political economist'.

I enter on this subject with a hesitation strong enough to have pre-
vented my entering upon it at all, did I not believe that to write for
or concerning women and avoid entirely that deplorable phase of
womanhood which, in country cottage as in city streets, in books,
newspapers and daily talk, meets us so continually that no young
girl can long be kept in ignorance of it, is to give a one-sided and
garbled view of life . . . Ignorance—quite a different thing from
innocence—is at once both helpless and dangerous.[12]

The sharp distinction between innocence and ignorance continued to be made—and offered as a new contribution to thought
—at intervals throughout the next decade.* Women were once
again appealed to by Mrs. Craik—to have more faith in themselves, to extend to the unchaste their 'unqualified, unmitigated
pity' and to abandon their customary attitude of 'God may forgive you but we never can'. Mrs. Gaskell's influence, after five
years, was still strong—for Mrs. Craik stressed once again the
importance of the child as a means of redemption and went so
far as to express her belief that no sin, 'not even this sin', necessarily corrupted the whole character. In this assertion she had the
support of A Lady (unnamed) who had told her that of the

---

* The issue was considered again in the *Westminster Review* of 1864
in an article 'Novels with a Purpose'—with reference to novels dealing
with the subject of prostitution. 'The best justification for such novels,
destined for general reading, assuredly is that women may perhaps be
redeemed from the possibility of remaining in that imbecile and ignorant condition which the romanticist commonly regards as innocence and
which woman is so generally encouraged to regard as her special virtue,
even by those who are so earnest in describing it as the principal cause
of her ruin.'

Vide, also, Trollope's Preface to *The Vicar of Bullhampton* (1869).

women who fell, many were much more refined, intelligent, truthful and affectionate than their fellows.

I don't know how it is—whether their very superiority makes them dissatisfied with their own rank—such brutes or clowns as labouring men often are!—or whether, though this will shock many people, other virtues can exist and flourish entirely distinct from and after the loss of that which we are accustomed to believe the indispensable, prime virtue of our sex—chastity. I cannot explain it!

Mrs. Browning saw no reason to explain it. She was perfectly clear in her own mind that the chastity of the body was unimportant in comparison with chastity of soul, and with some *élan* stated her viewpoint in *Aurora Leigh* (1856). Marian, after her violation, seemed as pure to Aurora as ever before. Purer, if possible. And although, in that case, there was no need to think of her child as a means of redemption, Marian chose to consider it her claim to happiness. Mrs. Browning, it could be seen, was no devotee of the 'Marriage makes an honest woman of her' cult. Marian, with a shake of her 'impassioned, spaniel head', gratefully refused Romney's offer of marriage:

> . . . Here's a hand shall keep
> For ever clean without a marriage ring,
> To tend my boy . . .

In only one particular might it be said that Mrs. Browning was lagging a shade behind her decade. The innocence-ignorance issue appeared to have passed her by. Or so the conversation between Marian and her mistress would indicate—a conversation which revealed no over-development of Marian's powers of observation and deduction.

> 'I think thou mock'st me and my house,' she said;
> Confess, thou'lt be a mother in a month,
> Thou mask of saintship.'
>   'Could I answer her?
> The light broke in so; it meant *that* then, *that*?
> I had not thought of that, in all my thoughts,—
> Through all the cold, numb aching of my brow,
> Through all the heaving of impatient life
> Which threw me on death at intervals—through all
> The upbreak of the fountains of my heart
> The rains had swelled too large; it could mean *that*?'

About this time the question of wild oats began to crop up in the novel more and more frequently and helped to forge in the minds of the public the fragile link between man's self-indulgence and women's ruin. 'Should wild oats be sown or not?' —such was the problem that authors coped with in their own, various ways. Coventry Patmore was commendably succinct:

> Who is the happy husband? He
> Who, scanning his unwedded life,
> Thanks Heaven with a conscience free
> 'Twas faithful to his future wife.[13]

Thackeray devoted a little more space to the matter. In *The Newcomes* (1855), just as Ethel is being reproved by Lord Kew for her youthful indiscretions, an anonymous letter arrives for her, in which are full details of her lover's past dissipation. Ethel impulsively confronts Kew with the letter, and for a moment it seems as if Thackeray is going to take up a definite moral standpoint at last. 'The young gentleman hung his head with sorrow over that sad detail of his life and its follies. What would he have given to be able to say, "This is not true." ' What he did say, however, put Ethel very neatly in the wrong: ' "My dear," he said, "if you had loved me you would never have shown me that letter." It was his only reproof.'

In Thackeray's opinion, then, Kew was still in a position to reprove. It was a great pity that wild oats were sown at all—but once sown, they should be forgotten and young ladies should not be too exacting of their lovers and husbands. When Mrs. Pendennis suspects that her son has seduced Fanny Bolton, her reaction is an idealistic one:

> 'Honourable! said the widow, with bitter scorn. 'Oh, brother, what is this you call honour? If my boy has been guilty he must marry her. I would go down on my knees and pray him to do so.'
> 'Good God! are you mad?' screamed out the Major . . .[14]

Thackeray's sympathies are in this case with the Major. Un-worldliness can go too far—and Warrington's life, hopelessly blighted as the result of a disastrous marriage at the age of eighteen with an ignorant country girl, is cited as proof of this. Miss Matilda Betham-Edwards, on the other hand, a minor but very popular Victorian novelist, took up a sterner viewpoint. If there were going to be any sowing of wild oats in her novels, redress must be made. In full. And preferably with marriage. In *The White House by the Sea* (1857), the scandal of the village was the return from abroad of a rich, middle-aged man to marry the girl he had wronged in his youth.

She was of humble birth and the world smiled on the young, rich, handsome Mr. Sterling and glossed over his fault . . . while the father died of a broken heart and the mother, goaded almost to insanity by her child's humiliation, set off on foot to some friends in Scotland and died on the way of weariness and want.

With two deaths and a seduction on his conscience, Mr. Sterling might reasonably have expected some show of approval from society when he made his delayed atonement. But no! 'Some crimes the world never censures; some virtues it never forgives,' was the comment of the disillusioned novelist. If we are to believe Miss Betham-Edwards, marriage out of one's class was, in the year 1857, for men, what loss of reputation still was for women.

The wild oats motif was given even more publicity when, in 1859, it formed the main theme of Meredith's novel *The Ordeal of Richard Feverel*. But no definite solution was to be expected from Meredith; he declined to come to any satisfactory conclusion. It was a big subject and it was quite enough for him to walk delicately round it, inspecting it from all angles. His indecision was once more not to Victorian taste and annoyed the critics. The *Westminster Review* asked, testily: 'What of the sowing of wild oats of which the novelist has so much to say? Are they to be sown or not, those wild oats? We do not feel that we are brought any nearer by the experience of Richard Feverel to the solution of that great social question about the sowing of wild oats.'

The fact was—no one quite knew. At any rate, no one felt prepared to express a settled opinion. Except perhaps George Eliot, who approached this subject of seduction with that moral earnestness which in great Victorian minds appeared so admirable, and, in small, so open to mockery. The circumstances of Hetty's downfall in *Adam Bede* (1859) were not unusual. The seduction of the village maiden by the handsome young squire had formed the backbone of many eighteenth-century novels. George Eliot may have been a little harder on Hetty than was the fashion in sentimental fiction: 'If a country beauty in clumsy shoes be only shallow-hearted enough, it is astonishing how closely her mental processes may resemble those of a lady in society and crinoline, who applies her refined intellect to the problem of committing indiscretions without compromising herself.'

And although she had the same opinion as Mrs. Craik about the superior refinement of country girls to men, she took care to give Hetty no such excuse for her ambitions, by providing Adam for her—Adam, who was far removed from the yokels that young Donnithorne mentions: ' "It's amazing what pretty girls one sees among the farmer's daughters, when the men are such clowns. That common round red face one sees sometimes in the men . . . comes out in the women of the family as the most charming phiz imaginable." '

None of the extenuating circumstances that George Eliot had deplored in *Ruth* were present in *Adam Bede*. It was, on the contrary, the motives prompting the deed that claimed her attention. It was the absence of the melodramatic in her treatment, her familiarity with the thought processes of Hetty and Arthur and the detached sympathy with which she viewed them that was new in *Adam Bede*. There could be no doubt as to the forces that urged the lovers on; sensuous, even more than sensual, attraction on Arthur's side, and vanity, ambition and passion on Hetty's. And for such primitive self-indulgence George Eliot could find no excuse, no real atonement. It was the doctrine of the irretrievable that she preached. 'There's a sort of wrong that can never be made up for', was Adam's conclusion. Neither seven years' exile and a rooted sorrow for Arthur, nor transportation and death for Hetty, could undo the harm caused to others by their misdeed. 'She's made our bread bitter to us for all our lives to come and we shall ne'er hold up our heads i' this parish nor i' any other.'

George Eliot had gravely placed her forefinger on what seemed to her to be the focal point of the morality tangle—lack of emotional self-control—and had condemned outright the sowing of wild oats by either sex. But *Adam Bede* could scarcely be

considered as a message of hope to any intending penitent. This
was supplied in the same year by a less distinguished contemporary, Henry G. Jebb, who produced in one volume a novel,
Out of the Depths, of which the *Westminster Review* wrote:

'If this book could be placed in the hands of those alone whom it is
calculated to benefit it might do some good; more indeed than the
cold exhortations to sin no more, professionally doled out by the
chaplain to those who come before him in the penitentiary or prison
. . . The great mass of female depravity which infests the streets of
English towns is not the result of seduction but of desire on the part
of women of no particular moral or mental cultivation, to escape
from the inevitable drudgery by which alone they can earn their
daily bread. There are multitudes just above the lowest class who
revolt from domestic service yet who, in the absence of sufficient
education, have no other resource than the needle; and yet it is not
in human nature to persist day by day in bending over the monotonous drudgery which makes the eyes prematurely dim and gives an
early stoop to the already delicate chest. To such the temptation to
vice is as strong as the inducements to continue chaste are to the class
which has all to lose by a dereliction from what is, in their case, as
much the path of interest as of virtue.'

From the outline of the novel it can be seen that the writer
kept his social purpose firmly in view throughout. Mary Smith,
the daughter of a head gardener on an estate, becomes engaged
to an Oxford undergraduate who is staying at the country house.
He dies before he can marry her; she becomes the mother of a
dead child and leaves home. Soon she is earning her living as a
prostitute, but, after sinking to the lowest depths, she experiences
a change of heart and is reclaimed, partly through the good
offices of a clergyman, partly through her own suffering and
self-denial. She becomes respected as a village school-mistress
and is about to marry a wealthy farmer who knows—but has
forgiven—her past when she becomes ill and dies. Redeemed, the
writer comfortably asserts, from all iniquities.

It was a new experience in the novel for the entire responsibility for the seduction to be accepted willingly by the heroine,
who told her own story with disarming frankness. If she had
not been eager to yield to her passion, her downfall would never
have been accomplished. If her lover had not died, he would have
married her and she would not have been forced to take the

somewhat considerable stride from early passion to prostitution. But Fate was not on the side of Mary Smith. And it is important to note that the heroine, in this case, was not, like Ruth, a guileless sinner on only one occasion, but a prostitute proper, a woman as degraded and debased as Mr. Jebb's capable pen could draw. And yet a woman who, as time passes, once more fills a position approximating to her earlier one.

The difficulties which attended the fallen woman who wished to secure employment were sympathetically recorded and the question of complete atonement handled bracingly. Although the heroine does, in fact, die at the end of the volume, it is made quite clear that marriage would have been as acceptable as death as a solution to the problem of the repentant Magdalen. Nor does Mary Smith have to go to the Bush to receive the offer, which she at first feels some reluctance in accepting.

'If I were not such as I am, Sir, I ought to be most grateful to God that such a man should wish to make me his wife; but the more I think of it, Sir, the more fixed I am in a solemn determination not to allow inclination and vanity to move me to do what honour and religion plainly move me not to do . . . I would defile the sacred name of wife.'

'But, Mary, if you were still as before—if you were not a truly repentant woman—what you have just said would be most proper and correct, but you are changed. Why should you thrust from you what seems to be of God's especial sending, to remove you perhaps out of all temptation, and to graft you again into that society which you once fell away from . . . If God has wiped away your soul's sins shall not man erase the memory of your body's sins?'

In the closing chapters the heroine and clergyman settle down to a comfortable chat on means of redeeming prostitutes, and Mary confesses that she does not think that refuges do any good to the 'higher grades of prostitutes'; that, in fact, she does not see that anything will, till a purer state of society exists and parents teach self-restraint and continence to their offspring, when young. 'It must begin with the young men, Sir, for as long as there are men to tempt there are women who will fall.'

'It must begin with the young men, Sir.'—It was a painful conclusion for Victorians to come to but one from which escape became increasingly difficult in the '60's, when Mrs. Butler and her followers really got down to their revelations. The end of this great, mid-Victorian decade saw, also, the end of the preliminary skirmishes for a single moral standard. A state of war was soon to be openly declared by the reformers. From now on the facts were to be told. National immorality was to be shown up. The path of the prostitute was no longer to be shrouded in darkness. The lights were going up all over England.

CHAPTER VI

Out of the Depths

1. THE STORM BREAKS

IT was Miss Harriet Martineau—ever mindful of brother James' early advice to devote herself to larger issues and to leave it to other women to darn socks and mend shirts—who broke the silence of her sex on matters moral. From her correspondence, in the *Daily News* of 1862, one of the first indications could be gained of the ethical storm that was gathering.

In that year, a Commission had been set up to look into the matter of venereal disease which had of late been ravaging the Army and Navy to such an extent that adoption of Continental methods of regulation seemed advisable. A fundamental change in England's ethical attitude was implicit in this proposal. Till then—apart from one or two brief lapses into tolerance—the country had pursued a rigid legal policy towards prostitution. Sexual indulgence was not condoned; keepers of disorderly houses were liable to prosecution; prostitutes could be arrested at any time. But attached as the nation was to its standpoint of aloof virtue, its health was a matter even nearer its heart. And if, by taking a lesson from the Continent on means of dealing with a disagreeable subject, it were possible to stop the rot—then perhaps moral superiority might for once be shelved.

But was it indeed possible to stop the rot by these means? Miss Martineau—who had studied the problem—thought not, and proceeded to explode the myth of the efficiency of the regulation system in four successive letters to the Press. Backing and confirmation from medical men, however, came too late and in 1864, amid general approval, the Contagious Diseases Bill* was passed.

To the public it appeared a straight issue between the health

* The Bill allowed the compulsory examination in certain towns of any woman suspected by the police of being a prostitute. If she were found to be diseased it authorised her detention for not more than three

of the nation and consideration of the feelings of prostitutes, although the immediate effect of the Act was not conspicuously gratifying. Prostitutes who objected violently, at first, to their fortnightly inspection were soon putting the clean bill of health they received to good use in attracting trade. A new and semi-official relationship sprang up between the police and brothel-keepers from whom information could be got about suspected prostitutes. Naval bases and regimental towns were given over openly to licensed viciousness. Hospitals were still flooded with cases and disease showed no tendency to decline . . . But through it all, despite facts and figures published, the public remained comfortably certain that the Acts were doing good. John Morley, writing in 1870, voiced the thoughts of many:

> To sacrifice the health and vigour of unborn creatures to the 'rights' of harlotry to spread disease without interference is a doubtful contribution to the progress of the race . . . This sentimental persistence in treating permanently brutalised natures as if they still retained infinite capabilities for virtue is one of the worst faults of some of the best people now living.[1]*

---

months in hospital. The Act was further strengthened in 1866 by the introduction of a periodical examination of known prostitutes under a well-organised system of medical police and in 1869 the maximum period in hospital had been extended to nine months. A measure of moral and religious instruction for the women when in hospital was advocated. Reference to this was made by Mr. William Fowler, in moving the Repeal of the Act in 1873.

'I have been shocked to read a great deal about the religious services carried on in the hospitals. The women are supposed to recite that prayer, praying to be delivered from fornication and all other deadly sins, while the whole cause of their being there is that they may be made clean to go out and commit fornication. Every woman knows very well that the intention of this Act of Parliament is to clean her up and make her fit again for this horrible business.' Hansard, May, 1873.

* Similarly, Lord Amberley, Jan. 1, 1870, in a letter to Mr. Newman, in support of C. D. Acts.

'I observe with regret that some of the opponents of the Act appear to devote their whole energy to securing the comfort and convenience of prostitutes and to be quite shocked if the feelings of this class do not receive every kind of consideration but to have little sympathy for the sufferings of the rest of the population from contagious disorders. . . . Of course, I argue on the supposition that the Act really would diminish the disease in question; if it could be shown that it would not, it would be worse than useless and I should surrender at once . . .'

Before Mrs. Butler and her followers—to whom there can be no doubt Mr. Morley was referring—came on the scene, in force, in 1869 there was here and there an isolated voice upraised in opposition to the Acts. In 1866, for instance, one Member of Parliament had objected to 'keeping public women at the public expense for the gratification of soldiers and sailors'—but the proposal by another member in the same year to punish any man who communicated a contagious disease to a woman was defeated. It was one thing to attempt to avoid reaping a disease-sodden harvest; quite another to infringe on the traditional right of men to sow their wild oats . . . But among intellectuals free speech on the subject of morality was growing far more common. In 1869, at a meeting of the Dialectical Society, there was an open discussion on prostitution at which one gentleman 're-joiced in the change of tone that had occurred since he began to write on this subject when he could hardly get anyone to discuss it. Now it was discussed here with ladies present'.

Not only with ladies present, moreover, but with ladies (middle-aged) taking an active part in the discussion. The views expressed were liberal. The onus of guilt was laid rather on men than on women, although sentimentalising over prostitutes was deprecated; both lack of employment and over-employment were suggested as reasons for immorality and mercenary marriages were condemned in the same breath as prostitution. 'Is there after all such a thing as morality?' one honourable gentleman was inspired to ask, as the evening drew to a close—but no one was prepared to take up the challenge. The question was a little too fanciful and philosophical for a realistic decade. The chairman, however, made a concrete enough contribution in his concluding remarks. 'He had heard', he said, 'a surgeon observe that prostitutes seemed to have all virtues but the single one of chastity'. No one, it might be thought, could speak fairer than that.

It was upon this assumption, certainly, that Mrs. Butler worked. The intellectual tea-parties and earnest young men of Oxford had long been left behind her. For years she had been labouring in Liverpool dockland among destitute women, setting up refuges for them, seeking them out in the huge damp cellars where they picked oakum in exchange for a night's lodging, visiting brothels each evening and carrying off the sick women she found there to die in comfort in her own home. Her compassion —and her husband's—achieved remarkable results, so that when she began her work in the larger movement for the repeal of the Contagious Diseases Acts she was armed with inside knowledge as well as hope. Under her influence—the influence Kingsley had envisaged of 'one real lady who should dare to stoop'— the Repeal movement was linked up with the other feminist campaigns and both men and women found themselves drifting together in pursuit of a common cause.

We have had experience of what we may call the feminine form of philanthropy, the independent, individual ministering, of too mediæval a type to suit the present day. It has failed. We are now about to try the masculine form of philanthropy—large and comprehensive measures, organisations and systems planned by men and sanctioned by Parliament . . . 'It is not good for man to be alone' was a very early announcement in the history of the world; neither is it good for man to work alone in any matter which concerns the welfare of the great human family.[2]

The agitators began to take action. In 1869 they published their manifesto,* propagated their views in their own newspaper *The Shield*, and in the following year, amidst great publicity, contrived the defeat at the Colchester election of the Government candidate who had asserted that 'prostitution should be recognised as a necessity to ensure the health of the Army'. Miss Martineau, the prophet without honour, having observed complacently the unparalleled scenes that were taking place all over the country, wrote to Mr. Butler:

How appalled the profligates are and how enraged! I have heard from very high authority that it is as if the depths of hell were stirred, so fierce is the passion of certain men at the check in a career which they had supposed would be made more secure . . .

* The manifesto was published in the *Daily News* and consisted of 8 clauses of which the fourth was that most frequently referred to:
'Because it is unjust to punish the sex who are the victims of a vice and leave unpunished the sex who are the main cause, both of the vice and its dreaded consequences; and we consider that liability to arrest, forced surgical examination and, where this is resisted, imprisonment with hard labour, to which these Acts subject women are punishments of the most degrading kind . . .'

The way of the *Pall Mall Gazette* and other newspapers of assuming
that the whole agitation was begun and is carried on by us women—
the men of all orders being left out of sight whenever possible—tells
volumes to my mind of their dread of what we may do and are
doing.[3]

Many opponents to Repeal, however, became supporters as
they listened to the repulsive evidence set before the 1870 Commission which was authorised to investigate the position. The
report, which followed upon their findings, started off bravely
enough with suggestions for diminishing prostitution by the
provision of primary education, moral training, increased opportunities for female instruction and better housing conditions
but came to grief in its conclusion. 'No comparison is to be made
between prostitutes and the men who consort with them. With
the one sex, the offence is committed as a matter of gain; with
the other, it is the indulgence of a natural impulse'.

Such sentiments were not only tactless. They were fatal.
Besides ignoring the fact of prostitution through economic
pressure, the report had contrived to give a resounding salute to
the double standard of morality. The Repeal group was not slow
to express its resentment and, after some dissension in the
thicker-skinned ranks, Bruce's compromise Bill of 1872-3 was
scornfully rejected by Mrs. Butler and her followers.* Their
disinclination to accept half-measures delayed repeal for over a
decade. For the next Government was sturdily united against
them and it was not until 1886 that the Acts of 1864 were at last
revoked.

What were the main issues that emerged from the *mêlée*?
What, in fact, were the Butler antiseptic doctrines which, applied
to the festering sores of the nation, drew forth such a bellow of
fury? Had the reformers been content to stop at moral salvage
the opposition would not have been so bitter. But, in their
opinion, the day of regeneration had dawned. The prostitute
must no longer be looked upon as so much wreckage floating
between the sexes—but as woman brought to her present state

* Mrs. Butler dismissed the new Bill with the remark that 'Satan
might sometime deceive us but not when he hides his cloven hoof so
clumsily.'

by man. The repeal of the Acts which degraded both sexes was only the first step. Next, the same chastity expected of women must be sternly demanded of men, both before and after marriage, as women's right.

But Victorians, on the whole, were still touchy where their private lives were concerned. It was just about this time that Amberley lost an election because he had expressed himself too freely in favour of birth control; it was scarcely to be expected that the outspoken remarks of the repeal group should be met with approval. It was true that progressive women, serious-minded working people and churchmen of all denominations supported the agitators. But on the other hand, it was not only Miss Martineau's 'profligates' who resented their interference. Many Victorians, who, as they stood, could have served as models for Patmore's 'happy husband', condemned the movement as unfeminine and unworthy. So that while, by 1873, a small, but representative section of the community could definitely be said to have been won over to the idea of a single moral standard for the sexes, the significance of the campaign, within this mid-Victorian period, lay rather in the fact that it brought moral problems to the forefront of the nation's consciousness than that it secured converts.

2. RECOMMENDED TO MERCY

During the '60's morality ceased to be a taboo subject for the novelist. With so much determined proselytising, so much discussion, so many revelations on all sides, lowered tones and guarded whispers became outmoded in the novel. And writers were not slow to realise that, if they had not quite been given *carte blanche*, they could at least—with sufficient moral earnestness to justify them—not go far wrong were they, in the course of their novel, to touch on an ethical issue or two. Morality, they found, held surprising possibilities.

Of late, the rake's progress through the novel had been considerably impeded by conscientious scruples on the part of authors; he had been forced to stumble where before he had swaggered bravely. But from 1860 onwards he presented an even sorrier spectacle. Mrs. Wood gave the decade a good start off with *East Lynne*. Victorians not only wept for the Lady Isabel but booed and hissed her seducer. With what painstaking care Mrs. Wood stripped the glamour from the handsome profligate: 'Captain Levison, unwashed, unshaven, a dressing-gown loosely flung on, lounged in to breakfast; these decked-out dandies before the world are frequently the greatest slovens in domestic privacy.' With what impassioned words she castigated him: 'Coward! Sneak! May good men shun him from henceforth! May his Queen refuse to receive him.'

Trollope, too, had no illusions and weighed out a generous measure of wretchedness to the wife of George Hotspur as a result of his vices. Even Miss Broughton, always a friend to passion and partial to a villain, could find no excuses for her fascinating, moustached Colonel Dare Stamer during his lifetime. Nor was death allowed to erase his sins, for the heroine, still clutching in her arms his lifeless body, expressed the reluctant opinion that he was bound for hell. Authors were coming out strong against the rake as marriageable material.

Reade was an exception. He chose to treat the matter with unworthy levity by making out a strong case for the reformed rake. That, in itself, would have been no new departure—had the rake not been of the feminine variety. 'Why should not women sow their wild oats also?' asked Reade, generously introducing an unlooked-for complication into an already subtle issue. And he proceeded light-heartedly to make out his case in *Hard Cash* (1863) by drawing Mrs. Archbold, the head of a lunatic asylum, —a woman who, he explained, would have continued wedded life as she began it, a good faithful and loving wife, had not 'the unutterable blackguard she had married, driven her, unwilling at first, to other men.' By the time our hero, Alfred Hardie, is trapped in her asylum, Mrs. Archbold is, however, no longer unwilling and there is no end to her amorous advances upon him. Even during the night he is not safe from the infatuated superintendent. 'And behold she held his hand between her soft burning palms and her proud head sank languidly on his shoulder and the inevitable tears ran gently.'

'Morals apart', added Reade appreciatively, 'it was glorious love-making.' Mr. Hardie, nevertheless, remains invulnerable to her attempts on his virtue and the news of her husband's death rouses her conscience. She turns her attention from him to a slightly weak-minded but very affectionate patient in the asylum and, neither young nor innocent nor virgin nor untouched by passion, becomes a model wife:

She made him as happy as the day was long . . . So, you see, a female rake can be ameliorated by a loving husband as well as a male rake by a loving wife.

It sounds absurd—and will offend my female readers and their unchristian prejudices, but that black-browed jade is like to be one of the best wives and mothers in England. But then, mind you, she always had . . . Brains.

The wives and mothers of England had, till now, shown no great inclination to throw membership of their society open to women whose brains made up for their lack of virtue, but Reade had effrontery enough for anything. Even he, however, would scarcely have dared to put forward such a suggestion had the English moral code not been in a sad state of upheaval and had novelists not been asking questions right and left. In the same year, for instance, a somewhat incoherent attack upon the marriage-form was made by Mrs. Norton in her novel *Lost And Saved*. In her dedication to Lord Essex she reminded him that 'I once jested with you as to your notions of charm and perfection in a woman and told you that I would one day create a heroine on that model and bring her to grief in a novel.'

The model of charm and perfection is brought to grief by a trick-marriage and is therefore in the eyes of Mrs. Norton, if not in those of the world, quite guiltless. The aim of the authoress was complicated. She did not set out to prove that love and not marriage was the important thing but rather to assail society for its intolerance of truly virtuous women—who appear bad by worldly standards—and for its tolerance of really bad women who appear virtuous because they are protected by marriage. At least, within her own novel, she was able to put the world to rights by marrying off her heroine to an Italian nobleman and disposing of her betrayer in a shipwreck. In this, some sacrifice was involved of her point that it was impossible for a woman of blighted reputation to rise again. But she could and did make herself clear when she expressed her opinion of the unjust moral judgements of the world: 'For though the faults of women are visited as sins, the sins of men are not even visited as faults. The day has not yet come either for the higher or lower classes in Great Britain when that vice which consists in the base behaviour of a man to one of the opposite sex is treated with any very marked severity.'

Meredith was equally concerned with the marriage form in *Rhoda Fleming* (1865), in which, with less elusiveness than usual, he heightened the 'honest woman' theme to a tragic issue and attacked the conventional belief that any marriage at all was better than none as a remedy for dishonour.

Dahlia, Rhoda's sister, is deserted by her lover, Edward, after solemn promises of marriage, and, while she is recovering from brain fever, she allows herself to be persuaded by her sister and father into marriage with a plausible scoundrel. Edward has, in the meantime, discovered that his intentions are honourable, but Rhoda will allow her sister's seducer to have nothing to do with her 'redemption'. The marriage is, in fact, illegal, but before this is discovered Dahlia has attempted to poison herself and, although she is dragged back to linger on for seven more years, she dies without becoming her lover's wife.

She had gone through fire, as few women have done in like manner, to leave their hearts among the ashes; but with that human heart she left regrets behind her . . . When she died she relinquished nothing . . . Almost her last words, spoken calmly, but with the quiver of breath resembling sobs were: 'Help poor girls.'

Despite Dahlia's last exhortation, the problem in *Rhoda Fleming* was not reduced, as in so many contemporary novels, to philanthropic terms. Like Hardy later, Meredith contrived to convey a sense of fatality, of the pity of it. The father's motive for pressing for marriage was worldly shame. Rhoda, on the other hand, acts out of disinterested love and the conviction that she knows best. But an ironical light plays upon their rigid respect for the form of marriage as Dahlia, ill and wretched, is supported from the altar into her father's presence:

For some few painful moments the farmer could not speak, and his hand was raised rejectingly. The return of human animation to his

heart made him look more sternly than he felt; but he had to rid
himself of one terrible question before he satisfied his gradual desire
to take his daughter to his breast. It came at last; like a short roll of
drums, the words were heard—

'Is she an honest woman?'

'She is,' said Rhoda.

It is not long before the full misery of her state as an honest
woman breaks in upon Dahlia, and the phrase begins to have a
hollow ring, even in the ears of the staunch-principled Rhoda.

'What am I tied to?' Dahlia struggled feebly as against a weight of
chains. 'Oh! what am I tied to? It's on me, tight like teeth. I can't
escape. I can't breathe for it. I was like a stone when he asked me—
marry him—loved me!—someone preached—my duty! I am lost, I
am lost! Why? you girl!—Why?—What did you do? Why did you
take my hand when I was asleep and hurry me so fast? What have I
done to you? Why did you push me along? . . . Hear me. I love
him; I love my lover and'—she screamed out—'he loves me . . . You
deceived me.'

Rhoda did not answer. In trying to understand why her sister
should imagine it, she began to know that she had in truth deceived
Dahlia. The temptation to drive a frail human creature to do the
thing which was right, had led her to speak falsely for a good purpose.

Another legal aspect in which novelists interested themselves
from time to time was that of illegitimacy. One of the objections
raised by George Eliot against *Ruth* had been that Mrs. Gaskell
over-emphasised the importance of legitimacy. The hysterical
scene, in which Ruth revealed to her small son the facts of his
birth, she felt to be strained and false when 'the least reflection
will tell Mrs. Gaskell that in our day no such brand affects the
illegitimate child.' In *No Name* (1862), Wilkie Collins took up
the point and showed how not only the fortunes but also the
outlook and character of his heroine, Magdalen, were changed
by the revelation that her parents had been unmarried. But
although Collins got his full dramatic effect out of the cruelty of
the legal penalty that made her 'an outcast of the whole social
community; places her out of the pale of the Civil Law of
Europe', it is unlikely that the social drawbacks of illegitimacy

were quite so drastic.* It is not to Collins that we must look for a temperate and faithful picture of the age, but to Trollope— and he appeared to be unaware of the fact that, by making his much admired heroine, Mary Thorne, poor and illegitimate, he was jeopardising her place in the gallery of Victorian young ladies. It was not so much from past lapses that Victorians shrank as from actual contact with present immorality.

They not only shrank from the more sordid and miserable aspects of prostitution, however. The stress laid by most writers on the poverty and wretchedness of the prostitute's life would render unaccountable the aversion and lack of sympathy displayed by respectable Victorian matrons had we no knowledge of a reverse side to the picture. Women could not be expected to digest without some discomfort the humiliating fact that, for some husbands, the *demi-monde* had an appeal that their placid home life was powerless to counter. There were bright lights in the *demi-monde* as well as darkness and shadows; fashionable clothes and bursts of laughter as well as rags and sighs. These were the allurements that caused acidulous, unforgiving attitudes in middle-class wives and inspired them with envy, fear, suspicion, hatred rather than with pity.

An article in the *Westminster Review* of 1864 put the matter bluntly:

It is discovered that throughout the English social life immorality is a much more general institution than successful and satisfactory marriage. Leading newspapers have admitted grave and earnest arguments to prove that the mistress is a far cheaper and more convenient companion than the wife . . . Anonyma is to a certain extent the pet of the age and is openly pleaded for by many practical moralists as a present necessity to the convenience and harmony of the world. But as no one has the courage to say that he thinks Anonyma a desirable institution in herself it is but natural that we should all incline much to the consideration of how Anonyma may be most promptly got rid of.[4]

Five years later, the bombshell which Mrs. Lynn Linton dropped on society, in the form of her essays, *The Girl of the*

---

* The illegitimacy of Esther Summerson, in *Bleak House,* is treated by Dickens with kid gloves, but he makes no melodramatic capital out of it.

Period, left what she described as the 'former ideal of woman-hood'—the fair young English girl—'generous, frank, refined, capable, modest, trustworthy, domestic, graceful, brave and brown-haired'⁵—suffering from severe shock. She was now, in Mrs. Linton's opinion, only a weak imitation of the queen of the *demi-monde.* She dyed her hair, painted her face, her sole idea of life was fun, her sole aim luxury, she followed extravagant fashions, indulged in slang and bold talk, was intolerant of morals and gave a general impression of fastness. Not surprisingly, there is no novel heroine to tally on all counts with such a description—but several of the features of Mrs. Linton's Girl of the Period are familiar attributes of heroines of Miss Rhoda Broughton. Such passages as these, from *Cometh up as a Flower,* give colour to Trollope's considered observation that 'she has made her ladies do and say things which ladies would not do and say. They throw themselves at men's heads and, when they are not accepted, only think how they may throw themselves again.'

The heroine, Nell L'Estrange, is surveying herself in the mirror before a ball:

'I'm coming, pa,' responded I, still making passes at the pale rose-filleted head I saw there. 'Ugh, you fright! There's pa calling again. Where are my gloves? Oh, Heavens, where can they have got to? Yes, pa, this very minute. What a potato face! It can't be helped. I *must* go.' Thus ejaculating, I *élancéd* myself downstairs.

Mercy Pecksniff had indulged in a somewhat similar style of jargon many years earlier, but while Dickens made no claim for Mercy's being a lady, Miss Broughton's heroines never let the readers forget for a moment that they are gently bred:

I laughed. 'Papa,' I said, 'if I were dressed in sackcloth and ashes or in the brim of a hat and spurs, I should look more like a lady than those great bouncing dairymaids, and, after all, that's all that matters.'

There is no doubt, too, that the Broughton heroines gave 'a general idea of fastness'—'Good God! How happy I was lying in his arms and with the top of my tall wreath scratching his handsome nose.'

As for extravagant fashions in dress, Mrs. Linton held no

brief either for the *outré* or the unfeminine. The bloomer, in
especial, she held in disfavour.* There are not many novels
centring upon a feminist dress fashion, but Reade, in *The Course
of True Love*, had, some years earlier, used as the crux of his
story his heroine's determination to wear the bloomer, in spite
of her fiancé's protests against her doing what 'three-quarters of
her sex think indelicate'. Their marriage is postponed by their
quarrel, but Caroline carries the day when she saves Reginald
from drowning—because she can not only swim (in itself an
'advanced' accomplishment) but is also unhampered by heavy
skirts.

'He can't swim,' cried Caroline, and she darted out into the stream
like a water-spaniel. In two strokes she was beside him and seized
him by the hair. One stroke took her to the remnant of the bridge.
'Lay hold of that, Reginald,' she cried. He obeyed, and while she
swam ashore he worked along the wooden bridge to the bank.
The moment she saw him safe, she began to laugh and then what
does my lady do but set off running home, full pelt, before he could
say a word to her. He followed her, crying, 'Caroline! Caroline!' It
was no use—she was in her Bloomer and had the start and ran like a
doe.[6]

A rescued hero instead of a rescued damsel provided a solution to the dilemma which, if not traditional, at least satisfied
Reade's sense of the fitness of things.

But, however sprightly and passionate Miss Broughton's Kate
and Nell and Esther, however athletic and independent Reade's
Caroline, they fall considerably short of the sum total of iniquities computed by Mrs. Linton and certainly do not give the
impression of being weak imitations of *demi-mondaines*. That
there was, in fact, such an attitude of rivalry is substantiated by
a short passage in William Black's novel of 1869, *In Silk Attire*.

'What a singular social life you lead in England,' cried Gersbach.
'There is the demi-monde, for instance. Why you talk of that and
your writers speak of it as if there were an acknowledged rivalry
between the members of it and your married women.'

* Writing of Dr. Mary Walker c.1870, she observed: 'I may as well
say here that the bloomer costume which she wore, with that huge rose
in her hair as her sign of sex, did much to retard the Woman Question
all round.'

'But our married women,' said Will, 'are going to form a trades union among themselves to crush that institution.'

At which Frans Gersbach looked puzzled. The English were capable of trying any mad expedient.

It was, however, a married woman who gave the best contemporary picture of the allurements of the *demi-monde* in a minor novel, *Recommended to Mercy* (1862). The heroine, 'considering the ceremony of marriage one of the most absurd inventions of mortal man',* braves society, lives with the man she loves, is abandoned by him and redeems her error of judgement by a life devoted to unwearying benevolence among prostitutes. There is no doubt in her mind that she has committed a sin, but it is a sin of her own choosing and her atonement is equally her own; upon the merits of her life as a whole she expects to be judged. So that it is not as a repentant Magdalen that the authoress puts forward her heroine, Helen Vaughan, for consideration, but as a mature woman whose character, needless to say, has been enriched by past suffering.

As in *Out of the Depths*, the heroine finds it practically impossible to find a situation once her past is known, and is given rational advice by her friend, an Archdeacon, to keep quiet about her expiated sin. ' "I consider," he said, "that there comes a time (after deep repentance and expiation) when a fault may be pardoned and its punishment cease. And does that punishment cease if we blazon to the world that woman's error on which of all others society has least mercy?" '7

The prostitutes, among whom Helen works, are neither forsaken nor forlorn, but gay, beautiful, fêted young women to whose repartee and complaisant services men of fashion turned as a matter of course. But although Mrs. Houston draws them in the zenith of their power, she loyally abides by trade union

---

* The disastrous consequences of free marriage formed a recurrent theme in the novel e.g. in novels as widely separated as Mrs. Opie's *Adeline Mowbray* (1805) and two productions of 1895—Grant Allen's *The Woman Who Did* and Thomas Hardy's *Jude the Obscure* (where Hardy uses it as one of the strands of his tragedy). The weary recantation made by Mrs. Opie's free-thinker on her death-bed—'The difficulty of divorce is one of the greatest blessings of mankind'—gives a fair indication of the life of torture undergone by the social rebel, whether Godwinian or late-Victorian.

rules in providing numerous warning pictures of them when they
are overtaken by disease or insanity. The heroine acts as the con-
necting link between the 'good' world and the 'bad'. Reclama-
tions seldom take place unless illness or want has overtaken
them, and many sick-bed changes of heart are distressingly temporary. One 'saucy little sinner, Kate Reilly', for instance—'a
joyous Irish girl, dark-eyed, sunny faced'—is still unrepentant at
the end of volume three, with very decided views on the 'ladies
who make us what we are'. ' "They envy us . . . Don't I see
how they look at us in the Park, how they dress after us, talk
like us, ride like us? They see we have the men they want, the
money they want and the fashion they want." '

There is much grave discussion between Mrs. Vaughan and
a doctor upon the best means of remedying prostitution. She
suggests that other interests for young women besides that of
obtaining a husband and bringing up a family would improve
the mental attitude, while better housing to avoid the mingling
of the sexes in 'one small room in a hideous festering mass of
impurity and pollution' would do much to help, physically. But
no cure—not even the emigration panacea—will, she insists, be
effective unless it is undertaken in a hopeful spirit. And as long
as the virtuous of the sex held aloof there could never be any
such spirit.

'Women have, I fear, harder hearts than men,' said Helen, 'and will
never admit even the most repentant of Magdalens quite within the
pale of their companionship.'
'No, they would keep her just outside, doling out charitable words
which their deeds belied, God forgive them, for they that do such
things have much to answer for.'

3. THE PENDULUM SWINGS

As the Repeal campaign assumed definite shape and its revelations became public property, downright treatment of moral
issues became the general rule in the novel. In *Parson Garland's
Daughter* (1867), Mrs. Craik, who had earlier objected to the
habit of casting a romantic garment of beauty and innocence
over seduced heroines, fell into no such error. Her heroine was
a rosy, black-haired servant girl—pretty enough, but slatternly

and ignorant, who was first seduced and then married by Parson Garland's son. The father had been cherishing since the death of his wife an ideal of womanhood which he hoped his daughter-in-law would fulfil. But although he was shocked by his son's action, he sternly did his duty—took her into his home, educated her and finally grew fond of her. The motive force behind her transformation was not repentance so much as her love for her husband. The point driven home very firmly by Mrs. Craik being that, as long as Woman has a heart, there is still hope for her soul.

At times it is plain that the authoress was in some doubt as to which episode in her heroine's past—seduction or domestic service—was the less salubrious. But in the matter of her marriage she came out most creditably on the side of uncompromising justice.

'She was, I grieve to say, not only a poor, illiterate servant girl: but—my son seduced her before he married her.'

'What!' cried the lady, starting back in undisguised horror. 'And you were so misguided as to let him marry her?'

'Madam,' said the parson . . . 'The one thing that inclined me to forgive my son was that he did marry her.'

Mrs. Crux regarded him in blank astonishment.

'I never heard of such a thing. That is, of course, such things happen every day; we mothers of sons know that they must happen. It's a sad, sad matter, but we can't help it; we can only shut our eyes to it and hope that the poor lads will learn better by and by.'

It is interesting to note that Mrs. Crux's sentiments are an almost exact replica of Thackeray's twenty years earlier . . . 'Alas, the life of such boys does not bear telling altogether. I wish it did. I ask you, does yours?' But now the authoress had no sympathy to waste on the 'poor lads'. Mothers of sons had not the same appeal for Mrs. Craik as they had for Thackeray.

Like Mrs. Craik, Trollope treated the subject of seduction with realistic commonsense. But unlike her, he was averse to making the central figure of his novel a woman of doubtful reputation. He stated his purpose in writing *The Vicar of Bullhampton* (1870) both in his autobiography and in the Preface to the novel:

The novel was written chiefly with the object of raising a feeling of forgiveness in the minds of other women. I could not venture to

make this female the heroine of my story. To have made her such
would have been directly opposed to my purpose . . .[8] Cannot women
who are glad pity the sufferings of the victims, do something perhaps
to mitigate and shorten them? No fault is punished so heavily as
that fault by which a woman falls—the less faulty of the two offen-
ders . . . The life of hell to which we doom our erring daughters
when because of their error we close our doors upon them! But for
our erring sons we find pardon easily enough.[9]

Trollope dealt with his heroine, Carry Brattle, kindly but
firmly. She is presented as a lovely girl who has gone astray,
once, but who would now give a great deal to retrace her steps.
It is against the cruelty of the herd that turns and rends her
that Trollope mainly directs his wrath. Her sister-in-law is
allowed to express the common viewpoint.

'What business had she to be sister to any honest man? Think of
what she's been and done to my children who wouldn't else have
had nobody to be ashamed of. There never wasn't one of the Hig-
ginses who didn't behave herself—that is, of the women . . . I don't
know nothing of such women nor what is their ways and I don't want.
I never didn't speak a word to such a one in my life and I certainly
shan't begin under my own roof.'

In her sister's reflections, on the other hand, Trollope expressed his own opinions.

As the lost one lay there asleep, lovely though an outcast from the
dearest rights of womanhood, Fanny could not keep her mind from
wandering away in thoughts on the strange destiny of women. There
Carry lay, a thing said to be so foul that even a father could not endure to have her name mentioned in his ears! And yet how small had
been her fault compared with other crimes for which men and women
are speedily forgiven, even if it has been held that pardon has ever
been required.

Loss of chastity then, in 1870, while still a grave matter, is
no longer in Trollope's opinion the unforgivable sin. The
indication he gives of Carry's later life is in keeping with the
matter-of-fact policy that led him in the first instance to reject
the role of heroine for her. He makes it clear that a normal life
is possible for her—normal, that is, if she does not find unduly
discouraging the fact that her father will never cease to treat
her as his erring daughter, and that there is no prospect of

marriage held out for her. There is no doubt in his mind that
Carry will never quite be able to eradicate her early mistake,
however sincere her repentance.

No such temperate approach characterised the novel published by Wilkie Collins in the year 1873, *The New Magdalen*.
1873 was also the year of Bruce's compromise Bill, but there
was no question of half-measures in Collins' study of the social
position of a reclaimed prostitute. As a message of hope to penitents it may, indeed, have been less effective than a more luke-
warm vindication. It would have been an unusual prostitute who
could have found her prototype in the heroine—who was as ideal
a young woman (past apart) as one was ever likely to meet. But
as an avowal of belief in the possibility of remaining chaste in
spirit and soul after the body had been prostituted, it electrified
the Victorian reading public.

The heroine, Mercy Merrick, is first encountered as a hospital
nurse in a frontier village during the Franco-Prussian war. To
an Englishwoman, Grace Roseberry, whom she meets there, she
tells the story of her past. She has not only been a prostitute by
profession, but is illegitimate by birth and has served a term in
prison. While in a Refuge, however, her heart had been touched
by a sermon preached by a young clergyman, Julian Grey, and
after many vain attempts to earn her living honestly, she had
seized the chance of becoming a front-line nurse.

At this point the village is bombarded, Grace is wounded,
apparently mortally, and Mercy decides to wipe out the past and
to return to England in Grace's place, under the protection of
an unknown guardian, Lady Janet Roy.

From then on, Mercy's history is one of happy uneasiness in
the love of her guardian and Lady Janet's nephew, the same
Julian Grey, upon whom her virtues, beauty and depth of character (once again, as usual, the result of suppressed suffering and
sorrow) have made a deep impression. She is on the point of
confessing her deception when Grace reappears and a full ex-
planation is made. Grace's virtue, however, has to be content
with its own reward, for Lady Janet, with unchanged affection,
pursues Mercy to the Refuge, to which she has proudly withdrawn to work among the unrepentant, and pleads her nephew's
suit. And, after much hesitation and heart-searching, Mercy con-

sents to emigrate with him to begin a new life in a New World.

It can therefore be seen that where other novelists paused in doubt, Collins plunged enthusiastically forward. Others had, for heroines, unfortunate girls; he was content with nothing less than a prostitute, bastard and jail-bird. Others had lovely, innocent maidens; his Mercy was a strikingly beautiful woman, of whom, 'Judging by a certain innate grandeur in the carriage of her head and the expression of her large melancholy grey eyes, believers in blood and breeding will be apt to guess that this is another noble lady instead of an outcast of the London streets.'

Others who advocated forgiveness for past sins might, none the less, stop short of marriage; he left no doubt that Mercy's marriage was as much a favour bestowed as received, as an onlooker's acid comment indicated:

Lady Janet's visit to the Refuge was neither more nor less than to plead her nephew's cause as humble suitor for the hand of Mercy Merrick. Imagine the descendant of one of the oldest families in England inviting an adventuress in a Refuge to honour a clergyman of the Church of England by becoming his wife! In what times do we live!

All society was not, however, educated up to the Collins' pitch, as could be seen from an extract from Julian's journal after a ball given by Lady Janet in honour of his new wife.

'I really had no adequate idea of the rudeness and coarseness which have filtered their way through society in these later times until I saw the reception accorded to my wife The days of prudery and prejudice are gone by. Excessive amiability and liberality are the two favourite assumptions of the modern generation. To see the women expressing their liberal forgetfulness of my wife's misfortunes, the men their amiable anxiety to encourage her husband . . . to receive this sort of welcome emphasised by obtrusive handshakings, sometimes actually by downright kissing of my wife—and then to look round and see that not one in thirty of these very people had brought their unmarried daughters to the ball was, I honestly believe, to see civilised human nature at its basest conceivable aspect. The New World may have its disappointments in store for us, but it cannot possibly show us any spectacle as abject as the spectacle which we witnessed last night at my aunt's ball.'

11*

The days of prudery and prejudice might be past, but Victorian moral standards were shifting uneasily in their moorings and all sense of security was gone. The Cape of Good Hope and Bush tradition was still being upheld by as modern a Magdalen as Mercy Merrick, but she was shaking the dust of the Old World from her feet in an entirely different spirit from Dickens' repentant prostitutes. A great change had been wrought in moral judgements since *Oliver Twist* was condemned in high moral quarters in 1837. Formerly, everyone knew what to think about morality; now, no one was quite sure.

But although there was increased tolerance to past errors, and the maiden with the flawless reputation was yielding in interest to the woman with knowledge and even experience of evil, there was still relentless insistence on present virtue. With the death of the Prince Consort and the emergence of the Prince of Wales into society, the family ideal had been gradually lessening its grip on the nation. There was in consequence more, rather than less, bitter opposition to the dissipation which was again becoming fashionable. For those who formerly, safe behind the ramparts of home, had ignored such evils, found now that it was impossible to remain detached; and those—the philanthropists and feminists—who had long been struggling to establish a single moral standard, redoubled their efforts. As a result, the resistance of Victorians to ethical shocks, which had been so low in the '60's, was gradually increased. Progress was, however, slow. Hardy, who had been attacked in 1871 for basing his novel, *Desperate Remedies*, on the postulate of a gently bred girl becoming an unmarried mother, was still well ahead of public opinion in 1891, when he wrote *Tess of the D'Urbervilles*. Although he wrote that book under the impression that readers would find in it only 'what everybody now thinks and feels', he was disillusioned by the outcry that followed. Victorian sensibilities were bruised by the novel as a whole, and by his subtitle—'A Pure Woman Faithfully Presented'—in particular. Feelings ran high, and Tess was the topic of the season, just as Ruth had been forty years earlier. But there was a significant difference in the spirit of the age which fathered Tess from that which had given birth to Ruth. The discussion was now open; women showed an undisguised interest in the moral controversy that was raging; there was no chance of Tess being suppressed, like Ruth, as unfit reading for mothers. The easy dog-days of masculine tolerance of their own shortcomings were almost over, and the exacting feminine planet was in the ascendancy at last.

EPILOGUE

THERE is one inevitable result of shadowing the Victorian heroine through the first thirty-six years of her life and carefully noting every feminist trait. And that is that our perspective of the age must suffer a little and the growing pains of feminism assume the importance of a major operation.

It is a temptation to continue to look at the nineteenth century through feminist eyes—to consider the Industrial Revolution solely as the working women's charter, the Crimean War as a heaven-sent opportunity for nurses, the railway train as a conveyance for Social Science delegates, the Education Bill as the Girton Girl's concern, the evolution theory as a regrettable counter attraction to feminism, and Mr. Gladstone as the worst stumbling block of all.

And in much the same way, it is hard to dismiss those heroines who, in the foregoing chapters, have shaken a century's dust from their gowns to take brief precedence over the better known young women of literature. For it was only through their feminist connections that many of them emerged from their stack-rooms at all; and once these are severed, the heroines of Dickens, Thackeray and Trollope automatically resume their rightful status. Novelists are no longer judged by feminist standards; and even Miss Charlotte Yonge comes into her own once more.

But, on the other hand, as the age swings back into focus, the value of the airing given to these forgotten heroines of forgotten Victorian novelists should not be underestimated. For two things are quite clear. First, that the interplay between the feminist movement and the Victorian novel was far more considerable than any cursory reading of the great novelists alone would lead one to suspect: that all aspects of feminism had a certain contemporary effect on the novel; and that neither the appearance, the character nor the intellect of the heroine was proof against the insidious influence of emancipation.

A second conclusion can, however, be drawn of more general significance. There is no evidence at all, in the novel, of one widely shared Victorian ideal of womanhood. It is true that the minor novels reflected more precisely the social fluctuations in women's position, mainly because it needed less literary ability to handle a controversial theme successfully than to embark on anything more artistically ambitious. But that does not mean that the major novelists were either impervious to social tendencies or faithful to one retrograde feminine ideal. They were neither. The indirect effects of feminism showed themselves in their heroines, in both physique and character. From one or other of certain 'advanced' qualities, such as athleticism, indulgence in slang, tomboy spirits, a hearty appetite, physical well-being rather than actual beauty, frankness in admitting their love and forthrightness in speech, few of their heroines were immune—although we have to go to the subaltern ranks to find Miss Broughton incorporating, with her usual *élan*, all these features in her heroine. It was only natural that the better writers should show more discrimination and less susceptibility to suggestion—but the emancipating trend is there, in their novels, all the same.

At the same time, however, their individuality guarded against their heroines running too closely to type. Amelia Sedley is still, too often, put forward as the typical mid-Victorian heroine when, indeed, the truth is that she had very little contemporary appeal, and within the confines of Thackeray's novels alone was challenged by such diverse young ladies as Becky Sharp, Ethel Newcome and Beatrix Esmond. It would be possible, without too much difficulty, by collating the most common characteristics in the heroines of major novelists, to build up a composite Victorian heroine—small, gentle, large-eyed and loving. Her most striking resemblance would be to Dickens' feminine ideal, for, throughout all his prolific writings, his *idée fixe* about young women never varied. But she would be only a shadow figure at best, for in creating her, vital differences between heroines would have to be slurred over.

For her stature, for instance, we should have to measure, by the same yard-stick, Dickens' Little Women and Trollope's 'little brown girls'; for her gentleness, fuse together the deprecating modesty of Esther Summerson and the proud submission of Jane Eyre; for her large eyes, ignore any disparity in expression

between the 'fine eyes' of Maggie Tulliver and those of Becky
Sharp or Agnes Wickfield or Rhoda Fleming; and for her affectionate nature, give no precedence to the gallant, loving heart of
Lily Dale over the passionate homage of Lucy Snowe. The
greater Victorian novels did, in fact, produce greater varieties
of heroines than ever before. It is even dangerous to generalise
about the heroines of any one particular novelist—Dickens excepted. The Trollope heroine, it is true, had certain family re-
semblances from which it is easy to deduce Trollope's private
feminine ideal—but his dislike of obstinacy, strong-mindedness,
excessive learning, independence in women did not exempt his
heroines from any such traits. And what is true of the conservative Trollope is even more true of the other novelists. While
their own ideal of womanhood may have remained static and
unprogressive, their heroines, at least, suffered change and altera-
tion.

And so, at the end of this first unchartered stage of their
journey, we leave these Thursday's children, the Victorian
heroine and the Victorian woman. They still have far to go—
the heroine, if anything, the farther—but the lonely days are
over for them. From now on they have no need of company, for
they do not walk unescorted or unacclaimed. In 1837 they had
no idea of their goal. Now, in the year 1873, every signpost is
marked for them and all are pointing in the same direction.

CHRONOLOGY

(*Restricted to Novels referred to in Text.*)

1837-8	*Oliver Twist*	Charles Dickens
1838-9	*Nicholas Nickleby*	Charles Dickens
1839	*Deerbrook*	Harriet Martineau
1839	*The Governess*	Lady Blessington
1841	*Barnaby Rudge*	Charles Dickens
1843	*A Christmas Carol*	Charles Dickens
1843-4	*Martin Chuzzlewit*	Charles Dickens
1844	*Coningsby*	Benjamin Disraeli
1844	*Amy Herbert*	Elizabeth Sewell
1845	*Sybil, or The Two Nations*	Benjamin Disraeli
1847	*Jane Eyre*	Charlotte Brontë
1847	*Agnes Grey*	Anne Brontë
1847	*Shadows of the Clouds*	J. A. Froude
1847-8	*Vanity Fair*	W. M. Thackeray
1847-8	*Dombey and Son*	Charles Dickens
1848	*The Tenant of Wildfell Hall*	Anne Brontë
1848	*Mary Barton*	Mrs. Gaskell
1848	*The Half-Sisters*	Geraldine Jewsbury
1848	*Yeast*	Charles Kingsley
1848-50	*The History of Pendennis*	W. M. Thackeray
1849	*Shirley, A Tale*	Charlotte Brontë
1849-50	*David Copperfield*	Charles Dickens
1850	*Alton Locke*	Charles Kingsley
1850	*Olive*	Mrs. D. M. Craik
1852	*Lewis Arundel*	Frank Smedley
1852	*The History of Henry Esmond, Esq.*	W. M. Thackeray
1852-3	*Bleak House*	Charles Dickens
1853	*Ruth*	Mrs. Gaskell
1853	*Villette*	Charlotte Brontë
1853-5	*The Newcomes*	W. M. Thackeray
1854	*Hard Times*	Charles Dickens
1854	*Heart's Ease*	Charlotte Yonge
1855-7	*Little Dorrit*	Charles Dickens
1856	*The Daisy Chain*	Charlotte Yonge
1856	*It's Never Too Late to Mend*	Charles Reade
1856	*Very Successful*	Rosina Bulwer Lytton
1856	*The Gilberts and their Guests*	Julia Day
1857	*The Professor*	Charlotte Brontë
1857	*The White House by the Sea*	Matilda Betham-Edwards
1857	*Two Years Ago*	Charles Kingsley

1857-9	*The Virginians*	W. M. Thackeray
1858	*Dr. Thorne*	Anthony Trollope
1858	*Scenes of Clerical Life*	George Eliot
1859	*Almost a Heroine*	E. G. Sheppard
1859	*The Bertrams*	Anthony Trollope
1859	*The Ordeal of Richard Feverel*	George Meredith
1859	*Adam Bede*	George Eliot
1859	*Out of the Depths*	H. G. Jebb
1859	*Love me Little, Love me Long*	Charles Reade
1860	*Lovel the Widower*	W. M. Thackeray
1860	*The Semi-Attached Couple*	Emily Eden
1860	*The Mill on the Floss*	George Eliot
1860-1	*Great Expectations*	Charles Dickens
1861	*The Daily Governess*	Mrs. Gordon Smythies
1861	*The Young Stepmother*	Charlotte Yonge
1861	*Framley Parsonage*	Anthony Trollope
1861	*East Lynne*	Mrs. Henry Wood
1861-2	*The Adventures of Philip*	W. M. Thackeray
1861-2	*Orley Farm*	Anthony Trollope
1862	*No Name*	Wilkie Collins
1862	*A Maiden of our Own Day*	Florence Wilford
1862	*The Channings*	Mrs. Henry Wood
1862	*Abel Drake's Wife*	J. Saunders
1862	*Recommended to Mercy*	Mrs. Houston
1863	*Hard Cash*	Charles Reade
1863	*Lost and Saved*	Caroline Norton
1863	*The Story of Elizabeth*	Anne Thackeray
1864	*The Trial*	Charlotte Yonge
1864	*Passages in the Life of an old Maid*	I. C. K.
1864	*The Small House at Allington*	Anthony Trollope
1864-5	*Our Mutual Friend*	Charles Dickens
1864-5	*Can You Forgive Her?*	Anthony Trollope
1865	*Rhoda Fleming*	George Meredith
1865	*The Clever Woman of the Family*	Charlotte Yonge
1866	*Piccadilly*	Laurence Oliphant
1866	*Felix Holt*	George Eliot
1866	*The Belton Estate*	Anthony Trollope
1866	*Armadale*	Wilkie Collins
1866	*Wives and Daughters*	Mrs. Gaskell
1866-7	*The Last Chronicle of Barset*	Anthony Trollope
1867	*The Claverings*	Anthony Trollope
1867	*Two Marriages*	Mrs. D. M. Craik
1867	*The Village on the Cliff*	Anne Thackeray
1867	*Cometh up as a Flower*	Rhoda Broughton
1867	*Not Wisely but Too Well*	Rhoda Broughton

1867	*Sowing the Wind*	E. Lynn Linton
1868	*Love or Marriage*	William Black
1868-9	*He Knew He Was Right*	Anthony Trollope
1869	*Phineas Finn*	Anthony Trollope
1869	*Nigel Bartram's Ideal*	Florence Wilford
1869	*In Silk Attire*	William Black
1870	*Which is the Heroine?*	Nina Cole
1870	*Put Yourself in his Place*	Charles Reade
1870	*The Vicar of Bullhampton*	Anthony Trollope
1870	*Red as a Rose is She*	Rhoda Broughton
1871	*Sir Harry Hotspur*	Anthony Trollope
1871	*Influence*	Jane Brookfield
1871-2	*Middlemarch*	George Eliot
1872	*The Vicar's Daughter*	George MacDonald
1873	*The Eustace Diamonds*	Anthony Trollope
1873	*Not a Heroine*	Jane Brookfield
1873	*The New Magdalen*	Wilkie Collins

NOTES

CHAPTER I: GOOD WORKS

[1] Article on 'The Queen and the Female Aristocracy'. *The Court Magazine*. (1837.)
[2] *Deerbrook:* Harriet Martineau. (1839.)
[3] *Autobiography:* E. M. Sewell. (Longman, 1907.)
[4] *The Alderley Letters*, ed. Nancy Mitford. (Chapman and Hall, 1939.)
[5] Miscellaneous Pamphlets. *Experiences of a Workhouse Visitor:* Emma Sheppard. (Nisbet, 1857.)
[6] Quoted by E. Moberly Bell in *Octavia Hill*. (Constable, 1942.)
[7] *Sisters of Charity:* Anna Jameson. (Longman, 1855.)
[8] *Englishwomen's Journal*, September, 1864. Article by Bessie R. Parkes.
[9] *Memorials of Two Sisters, Susanna and Catherine Winkworth*, ed. M. Shaen. (Longman, 1908.)
[10] *Letters from Charles Dickens to Angela Burdett-Coutts (1841-65)*, ed. Edgar Johnson. (Cape, 1953.)
[11] *Harriet Martineau:* J. C. Neville. (F. Müller, 1943.)
[12] *Life:* Frances Power Cobbe. (Bentley, 1894.)
[13] *Bleak House:* Charles Dickens. (1852-3.)
[14] *Two Years Ago:* Charles Kingsley. (1857.)
[15] *Lost and Saved:* Caroline Norton. (1863.)
[16] *Not Wisely But Too Well:* Rhoda Broughton. (1867.)
[17] *Bleak House:* Charles Dickens. (1852-3.)
[18] *A Maiden of our Own Day:* Florence Wilford. (1862.)

CHAPTER II: THAT NOBLE BODY OF GOVERNESSES

[1] *The Alderley Letters*. (Chapman and Hall, 1939.)
[2] *The Character of Woman:* Richard Cobbold. (Saunders, Otley, 1848.)
[3] Quoted in *Blessington D'Orsay—A Masquerade:* Michael Sadleir. (Constable, 1933.)
[4] *Lewis Arundel:* Frank Smedley. (1852.)
[5] *Vanity Fair:* W. M. Thackeray. (1847-8.)
[6] *Quarterly Review*, December, 1848.
[7] *Agnes Grey:* Anne Brontë. (1848.)
[8] *Armadale:* Wilkie Collins. (1866.)
[9] *The White House by the Sea:* Matilda Betham-Edwards. (1857.)
[10] *The Westminster Review*, January, 1858.
[11] *The Eustace Diamonds:* Anthony Trollope. (1873.)
[12] Ibid.
[13] *The Young Stepmother:* Charlotte Yonge. (1861.)

Notes

14. *The Amberley Papers*, ed. Patricia and Bertrand Russell. (Hogarth Press, 1937.)

CHAPTER III: WOMAN AT WORK

1. *The Amberley Papers.* (Hogarth Press, 1937.)
2. *Higher Education:* Emily Davies. (Strachan, 1866.)
3. Letter from Tennyson, November 21, 1882.
4. *Yeast:* Charles Kingsley. (1848.)
5. Ibid.
6. *Middlemarch:* George Eliot. (1871-2.)
7. *The Mill on the Floss:* George Eliot. (1860.)
8. *Letter to Miss Sarah Hennel, 1858.*
9. Vide *Mrs. Brookfield and her Circle:* C. and F. Brookfield. (Pitman, 1905.)
10. *Central Society of Education* (2nd Pub. 1838): Lady M. Ellis.
11. *Englishwomen's Journal*, March, 1861.
12. *Mary Barton:* Mrs. Gaskell. (1848.)
13. *Ruth:* Mrs. Gaskell. (1853).
14. *Orley Farm:* Anthony Trollope. (1862.)
15. *In Silk Attire:* William Black. (1869.)
16. *Shirley:* Charlotte Brontë. (1849.)
17. *Mrs. Lynn Linton; Her Life, Letters and Opinions:* E. Soames Layard. (Methuen, 1901.)
18. *Which is the Heroine?:* Nina Cole. (1870.)

CHAPTER IV: THE RIGHTS OF WOMEN

1. *Why Are Women Redundant?* (*Literary and Social Judgements*): W. R. Greg. (Trübner, 1868.)
2. Article on Divorce, *Westminster Review*, October, 1864.
3. *Novels With a Purpose, Westminster Review*, July, 1864.
4. *The History of Pendennis:* W. M. Thackeray. (1848-50.)
5. *The Newcomes:* W. M. Thackeray. (1853-5.)
6. *The Virginians:* W. M. Thackeray. (1857-9.)
7. *Great Expectations:* Charles Dickens. (1860-1.)
8. *The Gilberts and their Guests:* Julia Day. (1856.)
9. *Letters of Anne Thackeray Ritchie*, ed. Hester Ritchie. (Murray 1924.)
10. *Memorials of Two Sisters*, ed. M. Shaen. (Longman, 1908.)
11. *Love me Little, Love me Long:* Charles Reade. (1859.)
12. *Nigel Bartram's Ideal:* Florence Wilford. (1869.)
13. Ibid.
14. Ibid.
15. *Felix Holt—A Radical:* George Eliot. (1866.)
16. *The Novels of Trollope:* J. Herbert Stack. (*Fortnightly Review*, February, 1869.)
17. *The Claverings:* Anthony Trollope. (1867.)
18. *The Small House at Allington:* Anthony Trollope. (1864.)

[19] *Life and Work of Mary Carpenter:* J. Estlin Carpenter. (Macmillan, 1879.)

[20] *The Eustace Diamonds:* Anthony Trollope. (1873.)

[21] *Passages in the Life of an Old Maid.* (Saunders, Otley, 1864.)

[22] *Phineas Finn:* Anthony Trollope. (1869.)

CHAPTER V: THE SOCIAL EVIL

[1] *Early Victorian England,* ed. G. M. Young. (O.U.P., 1934.)

[2] Letter of May 26, 1846, from Dickens to Baroness Coutts *et seq.*

[3] *Autobiographical Notes:* W. Bell Scott. (Osgood, McIlwaine, 1892.)

[4] *The Lieutenant's Daughter* (included in *Shadows of the Clouds,* pseud. Zeta): J. A. Froude. (1847.)

[5] Letter from Catherine Winkworth to Emma Shaen, March 23, 1853: *Memorials of Two Sisters.* (Longman, 1908.)

[6] *Recollections of George Butler:* Josephine Butler. (Arrowsmith, 1892.)

[7] Remark made by Mrs. Jameson. Quoted by Elizabeth Haldane in *Mrs. Gaskell and Her Friends.* (Hodder and Stoughton, 1930.)

[8] *National Review:* W. R. Greg. (1859.) Reprinted in *Literary and Social Judgements.* (1868.)

[9] *Ruskin; Rossetti; Pre-Raphaelitism,* ed. W. M. Rossetti. (George Allen, 1899.) Vide also *Pre-Raphaelite Tragedy:* William Gaunt. (Cape, 1942.)

[10] Ibid.

[11] *The Wife of Rossetti:* Violet Hunt. (Lane, 1932.)

[12] *A Woman's Thoughts about Women:* D. M. Craik. (Hurst and Blackett, 1858.)

[13] *The Angel in the House:* Coventry Patmore. (1854-6.)

[14] *The History of Pendennis:* W. M. Thackeray (1848-50.)

CHAPTER VI: OUT OF THE DEPTHS

[1] *Fortnightly Review,* April, 1870.

[2] Quoted in *A Victorian Champion of Sex-Equality—James Stansfield:* J. L. and Barbara Hammond. (Longman, 1932.)

[3] *Recollections of George Butler:* Josephine Butler. (Arrowsmith, 1892.)

[4] *Novels With a Purpose: Westminster Review,* July, 1864.

[5] *The Girl of the Period:* Mrs. Lynn Linton. (*Saturday Review,* March, 1868.)

[6] *The Course of True Love Never Did Run Smooth:* Charles Reade. (1857.)

[7] *Recommended to Mercy:* Mrs. Houston. (1862.)

[8] *Autobiography:* Anthony Trollope. (Blackwood, 1883.)

[9] Preface to *The Vicar of Bullhampton:* Anthony Trollope. (1869.)

INDEX

Printed in Great Britain by
BILLING & SONS LTD.
GUILDFORD AND LONDON